TREATMENT OF "BATTLEFIELD" DETAINEES IN THE WAR ON TERRORISM

Treatment of "Battlefield" Detainees in the War on Terrorism

Jennifer Elsea

Novinka Books
New York

Senior Editors: Susan Boriotti and Donna Dennis
Coordinating Editor: Tatiana Shohov
Office Manager: Annette Hellinger
Graphics: Wanda Serrano
Editorial Production: Maya Colmbus, Vladimir Klestov,
　　　　　　　　　　　　Matthew Kozlowski and Tom Moceri
Circulation: Ave Maria Gonzalez, Vera Popovich, Raymond Davis, Melissa Diaz,
　　　　　　　Magdalena Nuñez, Marlene Nuñez and Jeannie Pappas
Communications and Acquisitions: Serge P. Shohov
Marketing: Cathy DeGregory

Library of Congress Cataloging-in-Publication Data

Elsea, Jennifer.
Treatment of "battlefield detainees" in the war on terrorism / Jennifer Elsea.
　　p. cm.
Includes index
ISBN: 1-59033-769-7. (cloth)
1. Prisoners of war—United States. 2. War on Terrorism, 2001-3—Terrorists. I Title

KZ6495.E44 2003
341.6'5'0973—dc21　　　　　　　　　　　　　　　　　　　　　　　　　　　　2003011881

Copyright © 2003 by Novinka Books, An Imprint of
　　　　　　　　Nova Science Publishers, Inc.
　　　　　　　　400 Oser Ave, Suite 1600
　　　　　　　　Hauppauge, New York 11788-3619
　　　　　　　　Tele. 631-231-7269　Fax 631-231-8175
　　　　　　　　e-mail: Novascience@earthlink.net
　　　　　　　　Web Site: http://www.novapublishers.com

All rights reserved. No part of this book may be reproduced, stored in a retrieval system or transmitted in any form or by any means: electronic, electrostatic, magnetic, tape, mechanical photocopying, recording or otherwise without permission from the publishers.

The publisher has taken reasonable care in the preparation of this book, but makes no expressed or implied warranty of any kind and assumes no responsibility for any errors or omissions. No liability is assumed for incidental or consequential damages in connection with or arising out of information contained in this book. Any parts of this book based on government reports are so indicated and copyright is claimed for those parts to the extent applicable to compilations of such works.

This publication is designed to provide accurate and authoritative information with regard to the subject matter covered herein. It is sold with the clear understanding that the publisher is not engaged in rendering legal or any other professional services. If legal or any other expert assistance is required, the services of a competent person should be sought. FROM A DECLARATION OF PARTICIPANTS JOINTLY ADOPTED BY A COMMITTEE OF THE AMERICAN BAR ASSOCIATION AND A COMMITTEE OF PUBLISHERS.

Printed in the United States of America

CONTENTS

Preface vii

Chapter 1	Introduction	1
Chapter 2	The Law of War	7
Chapter 3	Treatment of Detainees at Guantánamo	37
Chapter 4	Congress' Role	51
Index		53

PREFACE

After earlier criticism from human rights organizations and many foreign governments regarding the determination that the Geneva Conventions of 1949 do not apply to the detainees held in Cuba, President Bush shifted position with an announcement that Taliban fighters are covered by the 1949 Geneva Conventions, while al Qaeda fighters are not. Taliban fighters are not to be treated as prisoners of war (POW), however, because they reportedly fail to meet international standards as lawful combatants The decision is not likely to affect the treatment of any of the detainees held at the U.S. Naval Base at Guantánamo Bay, Cuba, and is not likely to quell all of the criticism.

While earlier reports that the detainees were being treated inhumanely appear to be unfounded, some allied countries and human rights organizations are criticizing the President's decision as relying on an inaccurate interpretation of the Geneva Convention for the Treatment of Prisoners of War (GPW). The U.N. High Commissioner on Human Rights (UNHCR) and some human rights organizations argue that all combatants captured on the battlefield are entitled to be treated as POWs until an independent tribunal has determined otherwise. The Organization of American States' Inter-American Commission has ordered the United States to take "urgent measures" to establish the legal status of the detainees.

The Geneva Conventions of 1949 create a comprehensive legal regime for the treatment of detainees in an armed conflict. Members of a regular armed force and certain others, including militias and volunteer corps serving as part of the armed forces, are entitled to specific privileges as POWs. Members of volunteer corps, militias, and organized resistance forces that are not part of the armed services of a party to the conflict are entitled to POW status if the organization (a) is commanded by a person responsible for his subordinates, (b) uses a fixed distinctive sign recognizable at a distance, (c) carries arms openly, and (d) conducts its operations in accordance with the laws of war. Groups that do not meet the standards are not entitled to POW status, and their members who commit belligerent acts may be treated as civilians under the Geneva Convention Relative to the Protection of Civilian Persons in Time of War (GC). These "unprivileged" or "unlawful combatants" may be punished for acts of violence for which legitimate combatants could not be punished. Some have argued that there is implied in the Geneva Conventions a third category comprised of combatants from militias who do not qualify for POW status but also fall outside of the protection for civilians. These combatants may be lawful in the sense that they do not incur criminal liability for engaging in otherwise lawful combat, but they would not be entitled to privileges as POWs or protected civilians.

The status of the detainees may affect their treatment in several ways. The Administration has argued that granting the detainees POW status would interfere with efforts to interrogate them, which would in turn hamper its efforts to thwart further attacks. Denying POW status may allow the Army to retain more stringent security measures, detain accused members of terrorist organizations indefinitely, and try some detainees by military commissions for violations of the law of war.

Chapter 1

INTRODUCTION

After earlier criticism from human rights organizations and many foreign governments regarding the determination that the Geneva Conventions of 1949 do not apply to the detainees held in Cuba,[1] President Bush shifted position with an announcement that Taliban fighters are covered by the 1949 Geneva Conventions, while al Qaeda fighters are not.[2] Taliban fighters are not to be treated as prisoners of war (POW), however, because they reportedly fail to meet international standards as lawful combatants.[3] The President has determined that al Qaeda remains outside the Geneva Conventions because it is not a state and not a party to the treaty.[4] The decision is not likely to affect the treatment of any of the detainees held at the U.S. Naval Base at Guantánamo Bay, Cuba, and is not likely to quell all of the criticism. The Secretary of Defense has reaffirmed that detainees will continue to be treated humanely.

While earlier reports suggesting the detainees were being treated inhumanely appear to be unfounded, some allied countries and human rights

---

[1] See Brian Knowlton, Powell and Bush Split On Detainees' Status Applicability of Geneva Conventions at Issue, INT'L HERALD TRIB, Jan. 28, 2002, at 1, available at 2002 WL 2884164; Tom Shanker and Katharine Q. Seelye, Behind-the-Scenes Clash Led Bush to Reverse Himself on Geneva Conventions, N.Y. TIMES, Feb. 22, 2002, available at 2002 WLNYT 0205300064 (quoting unnamed senior official that Britain and France had warned they might not turn over suspects captured by their troops unless the Conventions are observed).

[2] See Mike Allen and John Mintz, Bush Makes Decision on Detainees, WASH. POST, Feb. 8, 2002, at A1.

[3] *See* Press Conference, Department of Defense, Secretary Rumsfeld and General Myers, Feb. 8, 2002, *available at* [http://www.defenselink.mil/news/Feb2002/t02082002_t0208sd.html].

[4] See Fact Sheet, White House Press Office, Feb. 7, 2002, available at [http://www.whitehouse.gov/news/releases/2002/02/20020207-13.html].

organizations are criticizing the President's decision as relying on an inaccurate interpretation of the Geneva Convention for the Treatment of Prisoners of War (GPW).[5] The U.N. High Commissioner on Human Rights (UNHCR) and some human rights organizations argue that all combatants captured on the battlefield are entitled to be treated as Jan Cienski, *Detainees' Families File Suit: Lawsuit Demands Legal Process for Two Britons, One Australian Held by the United States: Camp X-ray Prisoners*, NAT'L POST Feb. 20, 2002, at A13, *available at* 2002 WL 11861252. POWs until an independent tribunal has determined otherwise.[6] The European Parliament also called for a tribunal to determine the status of detainees.[7] Great Britain has reportedly asked that its citizens detained in Cuba be returned for trial.[8] A controversy ensued in Canada after it was reported that Canadian soldiers turned over several of their captives to the United States for detention, argued by some to be in possible violation of Canada's international obligations.[9] The Organization of American States' Inter-American Commission has issued a preliminary order to the United States, urging it to take "urgent measures" to establish hearings to determine the legal status of the detainees.[10]

The U.S. Justice Department has reportedly set up a special legal team headed by the Solicitor-General to defend its policy of holding detainees at Guantánamo Bay against court challenges brought on their behalf.[11] One

---

[5] The Geneva Convention Relative to the Treatment of Prisoners of War, August 12, 1949, 6 U.S.T. 3317 (hereinafter "GPW").

[6] *See Red Cross Differs on POWs*, DETROIT FREE PRESS, Feb. 9, 2002, at 6A (reporting International Committee of the Red Cross (ICRC) statement criticizing Bush decision); *Afghan Human Rights is Cause for concern, Warns Top UN Official*, AGENCE FRANCEPRESSE Feb. 12, 2002, available at 2002 WL 2338501 (reporting UNHCR Chief Mary Robinson agreed with legal position of ICRC regarding Geneva Conventions' applicability to detainees); Letter from Kenneth Roth, Executive Director Human Rights Watch, to Condoleezza Rice, National Security Advisor (Jan. 28, 2002) (available at http://hrw.org/press/2002/01/us012802-ltr.htm).

[7] *See Euro MPs Seek Tribunal to Determine Cuba Prisoners' Status*, AGENCE PRESSEFRANCE, Feb. 7, 2002, *available at* 2002 WL 2335140.

[8] *See* Sue Leeman, *Britain Wants Captives Tried at Home*, AP Jan. 24, 2002, *available at* 2002 WL 10035010;

[9] *See* Jeff Sallot, *Captives' Status Worries Ottawa*, GLOBE & MAIL (Ottawa), Feb. 5, 2002, at A4. Under the GPW, a Detaining Power may transfer captives to another Power only "after it has satisfied itself of the willingness and ability of such transferee Power to apply the Convention." GPW art. 12.

[10] *See* Jesse Bravin, *Panel Says U.S. Policy on Detainees in Cuba Breaks International Law*, WALL ST. J., Mar. 14, 2002, at B2.

[11] *See* John Mintz, *Guantanamo Could Be Terrorist Penal Colony; U.S. Preparing New Guidelines for Tribunals*, Sun-Sentinel (Ft. Lauderdale Fla.), Feb 13, 2002, at 19A, *available at* 2002 WL 2946820.

petition for *habeas corpus* was rejected by a district court in California on the grounds that the petitioner – a coalition of clergy and human rights lawyers – did not have standing to bring the action on behalf of all of the prisoners.[12] Another case was filed in the District of Columbia against President Bush and Secretary of Defense Rumsfeld by the parents of three of the detainees – one Australian national and two from the United Kingdom.[13] The Justice Department reportedly plans to ask the court to decline jurisdiction based on the Supreme Court decision in *Johnson v. Eisentraeger*[14] holding that enemy aliens have no right to have their cases heard in U.S. courts if they are not being held on U.S. soil. The court in the California case found that argument persuasive.

The Geneva Conventions of 1949 create a comprehensive legal regime for the treatment of detainees in an armed conflict.[15] Members of a regular armed force and certain others, including militias and volunteer corps serving as part of the armed forces, are entitled to specific privileges as POWs. Members of volunteer corps, militias, and organized resistance forces that are not part of the armed services of a party to the conflict are entitled to POW status if the organization (a) is commanded by a person responsible for his subordinates, (b) uses a fixed distinctive sign recognizable at a distance, (c) carries arms openly, and (d) conducts its operations in accordance with the laws of war.[16] Groups that do not meet the standards are not entitled to POW status, and their members who commit belligerent acts may be treated as civilians under the Geneva Convention Relative to the Protection of

---

[12] Coalition of Clergy v. Bush, No. CV 02-570 AHM (JTLX) (C.D. Cal. 2002), *available at* 2002 WL 272428.

[13] Jan Cienski, *Detainees' Families File Suit: Lawsuit Demands Legal Process for Two Britons, One Australian Held by the United States: Camp X-ray Prisoners*, NAT'L POST Feb. 20, 2002, at A13, *available at* 2002 WL 11861252.

[14] 339 U.S. 763 (1950).

[15] Geneva Convention for the Amelioration of the Condition of the Wounded and Sick in Armed Forces in the Field, opened for signature Aug. 12, 1949, 6 U.S.T. 3114, T.I.A.S. No. 3362, 75 U.N.T.S. 31 (entered into force Oct. 21, 1950); Geneva Convention for the Amelioration of the Condition of Wounded, Sick and Shipwrecked Members of Armed Forces at Sea, opened for signature Aug. 12, 1949, 6 U.S.T. 3217, T.I.A.S. No. 3363, 75 U.N.T.S. 85 (entered into force Oct. 21, 1950); Geneva Convention Relative to the Treatment of Prisoners of War, opened for signature Aug. 12, 1949, 6 U.S.T. 3316, T.I.A.S. No. 3364, 75 U.N.T.S. 135 (entered into force Oct. 21, 1950); Geneva Convention Relative to the Protection of Civilian Persons in Time of War, opened for signature Aug. 12, 1949, 6 U.S.T. 3516, T.I.A.S. No. 3365, 75 U.N.T.S. 287 (entered into force Oct. 21, 1950) [hereinafter referred to collectively as the "1949 Geneva Conventions" or "Conventions"].

[16] GPW art. 4A(2).

Civilian Persons in Time of War (GC).[17] These "unprivileged" or "unlawful combatants" may be punished for acts of violence for which legitimate combatants could not be punished.[18] Some have argued that there is implied in the Geneva Conventions a third category comprised of combatants from militias that do not qualify for POW status but also fall outside of the protection for civilians. These combatants may be lawful in the sense that they do not incur criminal liability for engaging in otherwise lawful combat, but they would not be entitled to privileges as POWs or protected civilians.[19]

The status of the detainees may affect their treatment in several ways. The Administration has argued that granting the detainees POW status will interfere with efforts to interrogate them, which would in turn hamper its efforts to thwart further attacks. Denying POW status may allow the Army to retain more stringent security measures, including close confinement of detainees in prison-like cells. The Administration also argues that the detainees, if granted POW status, would have to be repatriated when hostilities in Afghanistan cease, freeing them to commit more terrorist acts. Finally, POWs accused of crimes are entitled to trial by court-martial or regular civil court. Denying POW status would appear to leave open the possibility that the detainees may be tried by military commissions for violations of the law of war.[20]

The White House has not yet issued a legal opinion to clarify its application of the GPW to the Taliban, whose members would arguably seem to be eligible for POW status as members of the armed forces of Afghanistan under a plain reading of GPW art. 4A(1). It has been suggested that the four criteria in GPW art. 4A(2) apply to regular armed forces as a

---

[17] Geneva Convention Relative to the Protection of Civilian Persons in Time of War, Aug. 12, 1949, 6 U.S.T. 3516, T.I.A.S. No. 3365, 75 U.N.T.S. 287 (hereinafter "GC").

[18] *See* Maj. Richard R. Baxter, *So-Called 'Unprivileged Belligerency': Spies, Guerrillas, and Saboteurs,* 28 BRIT. Y.B. INT'L L. 323,343 (1951) (explaining that belligerency is not violative of international law, but is merely unprotected by it).

[19] See W. Thomas Mallison and Sally V. Mallison, The Juridical Status of Irregular Combatants under the International Law of Armed Conflicts, 9 CASE W. RES.J.INT'L L. 39, 43 (1977) (suggesting a category of "other combatants, such as spies, saboteurs, and the irregulars who do not meet the applicable criteria of the law of armed conflict [who are] lawful combatants in particular contexts, but ... not entitled to privileged treatment of POWs upon capture.").

[20] Military Order, November 13, 2001 Detention, Treatment, and Trial of Certain Non- Citizens in the War Against Terrorism §1(a), 66 Fed. Reg. 57,833 (Nov. 16, 2001); *see* Terrorism and the Law of War: Trying Terrorists as War Criminals before Military Commissions, CRS Report RL31191 (updated Dec. 11, 2001).

matter of customary international law;[21] however, others point out that state practice does not appear to support the conclusion that the armed forces of states have been categorically denied eligibility for POW status on the basis that the army did not comply completely with the law of war. Indeed, U.S. practice has been to accord POW status generously to irregulars,[22] to support such status for irregular forces at times,[23] and to raise objections whenever an adversary has sought to deny U.S. personnel POW status based on a general accusation that the U.S. forces were not in compliance with some aspect of the law of war.[24] The Administration has also asserted that the Geneva Conventions are obsolete when it comes to dealing with terrorists,[25] but will continue to follow the treaties' principles.

With respect to al Qaeda fighters, the Administration has stated it is not applying the Geneva Conventions because al Qaeda is not a state party to the Geneva Conventions.[26] Opponents of that position argue that the Geneva Conventions do not apply solely to the armed forces of state parties to the Conventions; that the treaties also cover non-state belligerents, who have not been allowed to become parties to the Conventions. Partisan and other irregular groups can qualify for POW status if they otherwise meet the criteria in GPW art. 4. Non-states as well as states that are not parties to the Conventions remain bound by the provisions that have attained *opinio juris* status,[27] and may also accept the obligations of the Conventions in return for more favorable treatment. Common article 3 of the Geneva Conventions provides minimum protection during non-international conflicts for all captives.[28]

---

[21] *See* Mallison and Mallison, *supra* note 19, at 73 (describing procedures used during Vietnam conflict to determine status of Viet Cong fighters).

[22] *See, e.g.*, discussion about procedures adopted during Vietnam conflict, *infra* note 157 *et seq.*

[23] *See* HOWARD S. LEVIE, PRISONERS OF WAR IN INTERNATIONAL ARMED CONFLICT 40-41 (1979) (noting that during WWII, the United States claimed the Philippine resistance movement as an adjunct of its own armed forces).

[24] *See* D. SCHINDLER & J. TOMAN, THE LAWS OF ARMED CONFLICT 563-92 (1981) (reporting U.S. and allies' objections to Communist countries' reservations to GPW, which resulted in the failure of U.S. airmen to qualify for POW status in Korea and Vietnam conflicts on the basis they were "war criminals").

[25] *See* Rumsfeld Press Conference, *supra* note 3.

[26] *See* Press Release, White House, Status of Detainees at Guantánamo (Feb. 7, 2002) (*available at* [http://www.whitehouse.gov/news/releases/2002/02/20020207-13.html]).

[27] *See* Theodore Meron, *The Geneva Conventions as Customary International Law*, 81 AM. J. INT'L L 348, 350 (1987).

[28] The 1949 Geneva Conventions share several types of common provisions. The first three articles of each Convention are identical. Common Article 3, note 88, *infra*, has been described as "a convention within a convention" to provide a general formula covering respect for intrinsic human values that would always be in force, without regard to the

Another consideration may be that al Qaeda members would retain their status as citizens of their states of nationality. The status and treatment of prisoners of war generally does not depend on their nationality.[29] However, civilians would not ordinarily derive their status under the Conventions from membership in a private organization. Under this view, the relevant issue would be whether they are citizens of states that are parties to the Conventions and whether those states have normal diplomatic relations with the United States.[30] The President's decision regarding al Qaeda's status suggests that he may consider al Qaeda to have sufficient "international personality" to be a valid party to the conflict and subject to the law of war, but the White House has not to date issued a statement clarifying its position.

---

characterization the parties to a conflict might give it. *See* JEAN PICTET, HUMANITARIAN LAW AND THE PROTECTION OF WAR VICTIMS 32 (1975). Originally a compromise between those who wanted to extend the Convention's protection to all insurgents and rebels and those who wanted to limit it to wars between states, Common Article 3 is now considered to have attained the status of customary international law. *See* KRIANGSAK KITTICHAISAREE, INTERNATIONAL CRIMINAL LAW 188 (2001).

[29] *See In re* Territo, 156 F.2d 142 (9th Cir. 1946).

[30] *See* GC art. 4, which states, in part: Persons protected by the Convention are those who, at a given moment and in any manner whatsoever, find themselves, in case of a conflict or occupation, in the hands of a Party to the conflict or Occupying Power of which they are not nationals. Nationals of a State which is not bound by the Convention are not protected by it. Nationals of a neutral State who find themselves in the territory of a belligerent State, and nationals of a co-belligerent State, shall not be regarded as protected persons while the State of which they are nationals has normal diplomatic representation in the State in whose hands they are.

Chapter 2

THE LAW OF WAR

The law of war, also known as the law of armed conflict or humanitarian law, is a subset of international law that has evolved through centuries of efforts to mitigate the harmful effects of war. Recognizing the impossibility of eliminating warfare all together, nations in essence have agreed to abide by rules limiting their conduct in war, in return for the enemy's agreement to abide by the same rules.[31] There are two branches of the law of war: The older of the two branches, known as "Hague law" after the Hague Conventions of 1899 and 1907, prescribes the rules of engagement during combat and is based on the key principles of military necessity and proportionality.[32] The humanitarian side of the law, known as "Geneva law," emphasizes human rights and responsibilities, including the humane and just treatment of prisoners.

The legality and proper justification for resorting to war in the first place are a separate legal regime. A principal distinction exists between the law of conduct during war – *jus in bello* – and international law regulating when going to war is justified – *jus ad bellum*.[33] Parties to an armed conflict retain the same rights and obligations without regard to which party initiated

---

[31] *See* Mallison and Mallison, *supra* note 19, at 41(noting the law of war is dependent for its observance on the common interests of participants).

32 See PICTET, supra note 28, at 31 (describing the principle that "belligerents shall not inflict on their adversaries harm out of proportion to the object of warfare, which is to destroy or weaken the military strength of the enemy").

[33] *See* DOCUMENTS ON THE LAWS OF WAR 1 (Adam Roberts and Richard Guelff, eds. 2000)(hereinafter "DOCUMENTS"). 34*See* CIVILIANS IN WAR 16-17 (Simon Chesterman, ed. 2001) (explaining that theories of "just war" were to be kept separate from *jus in bello* in part to make it easier to maintain legal parity between parties, holding both sides to same rules of conduct).

hostilities and whether that conduct is justifiable under international law.[34] Otherwise, each party would routinely regard its enemy as unlawfully engaging in war and would thus feel justified in taking whatever measures might be seen as necessary to accomplish its defeat.[35]

If the law of war is to have any effect in restraining the conduct of belligerents, there must be both inducements for adherence to it and punishment for failure to adhere.[36] One incentive for parties to adhere to the rules is the promise that their members will receive humane treatment and some legal privileges at the hands of the enemy if they are captured. Reciprocity serves as a primary motivator, but is not an absolute requirement for adherence;[37] a derogation from the rules by one party does non-execution of a treaty by one party may ultimately release the other party from its obligations, or justify the annulment of the treaty, like a contract under municipal laws. This, however, would not apply to the Geneva Conventions: whatever the circumstances, they remain valid and are not subject to reciprocity. Indeed, the mind absolutely rejects the idea that a belligerent should, for instance, deliberately ill-treat or kill prisoners because the adversary his been guilty of such crimes not excuse breaches by another,[38] although reprisal in proportion may be permissible.[39] Were this not the case, any deviation from the letter of the law could be invoked to justify wholesale abandonment of the law of war, causing the conflict to degenerate into the

---

[34] See CIVILIANS IN WAR 16-17 (Simon Chester man, ed. 2001) (explaining that theories of "just war" were to be kept separate from jus in bello in part to make it easier to maintain legal parity between parties, holding both sides to same rules of conduct).

[35] *See* HILAIRE MCCOUBREY, 2 INTERNATIONAL HUMANITARIAN LAW 2 (1998) (predicting that the mixing of *jus in bello* and *jus ad bellum* "...would represent a renaissance of the very worst features of medieval 'just war' theory.").

[36] See Mallison and Mallison, *supra* note 19, at 41 (noting that the central technique for enforcing the law of war has been a system of interrelated rights and duties).

[37] *See* PICTET, *supra* note28, at 21 (1975): It is generally admitted that the non-execution of treaty by one party may ultimately release the other party from its obligations, or justify the annulment of the treaty, like a contract under municipal laws. This, however, would not apply to Geneva Conventions: whatever the circumstances, they remain valid and are not subject to reciprocity. Indeed, the mind absolutely rejects the idea that a belligerent should, for instance, deliberately ill-treat or kill prisoners because the adversary has been guilty of such crimes.

[38] *But see* LEVIE, *supra* note 23, at 31(stating that commentators appear to agree that "few states can actually be expected to continue to apply the provisions of the [GPW] in the absence of reciprocity despite the provision to that effect...").

[39] *See* THE HANDBOOK OF HUMANITARIAN LAW IN ARMED CONFLICTS 204 (Dieter Fleck, ed. 1995)(hereinafter "HANDBOOK")(defining *reprisals* as "coercive measures which would normally be contrary to international law but which are taken in retaliation by one party to a conflict in order to stop the adversary from violating international law.").

kind of barbarity the law of war aims to mitigate. Reprisals may not be taken against POWs or other protected persons.[40]

Some experts argue that in keeping with the purpose of humanitarian law, that is, to protect civilians and reduce the needless suffering of combatants, humanitarian law should be interpreted as broadly as possible in favor of individual rights and protections, to include rights of irregular combatants who comply to the extent possible with the law of war. Under this view, no one falls completely outside the protection of the Geneva Conventions during an armed conflict. Others would adhere rigidly to the letter of the law, denying rights to irregular combatants in order to deter the formation of resistance movements and to avoid legitimizing their belligerent acts. Proponents of this view argue the treatment of detainees not clearly covered by the Conventions is entirely at the discretion of the detaining power.

AUTHORITY TO DETAIN DURING WAR

The treatment of all persons who fall into the hands of the enemy during an armed conflict depends upon the status of the person as determined under the four Geneva Conventions of 1949. Parties to an armed conflict have the right to intern enemy prisoners of war,[41] as well as civilians who pose a danger to the security of the state,[42] at least for the duration of hostilities.[43] The right to detain enemy combatants is not based on the supposition that the prisoner is "guilty" as an enemy for any crimes against the Detaining Power, either as an individual or as an agent of the opposing state. POWs are detained for security purposes only, to remove those soldiers from further participation in combat. The detention is not a form of

---

[40] *See id.* at 206.
[41] *See* GPW art. 21: The Detaining Power may subject prisoners of war to internment. It may impose on them the obligation of not leaving, beyond certain limits, the camp where they are interned, or if the said camp is fenced in, of not going outside its perimeter. Subject to the provisions of the present Convention relative to penal and disciplinary sanctions, prisoners of war may not be held in close confinement except where necessary to safeguard their health and then only during the continuation of the circumstances which make such confinement necessary.
[42] GC art. 42 states: The internment or placing in assigned residence of protected persons may be ordered only if the security of the Detaining Power makes it absolutely necessary.
[43] *See* GPW art. 21; PICTET, *supra* note 28, at 47 ("Prisoners will be released and repatriated as soon as there are no longer any reasons for captivity, that is to say, at the end of active hostilities.").

punishment.[44] The Detaining Power may punish enemy soldiers and civilians for crimes committed prior to their capture as well as during captivity, but only after a fair trial in accordance with the relevant convention and other applicable international law. Failure to accord prisoners a fair trial is a grave breach under article 130 of GPW[45] and article 146 of GC.[46]

Neutral and non-belligerent signatory countries also have an obligation to intern members of belligerent armed forces under the Geneva Conventions of 1949.[47] The neutral country must treat these prisoners as POWs, except that certain provisions do not apply, including arts. 8, 10 and 126 (relating to visits by representatives of the Protecting Power[48] or international organization acting in that role), 15 and 30 (maintenance and medical care; in this case costs are to be borne by the belligerent nations), 58-67 (financial resources) and 92 (penal provisions for unsuccessful escape).[49] There is no express obligation to arrest and detain persons who are not lawful combatants and are suspected of having participated in hostilities before crossing a border into neutral territory.

---

[44] *See* PICTET, *supra* note 28, at 46.

[45] GPW art. 130 states: Grave breaches to which the preceding Article relates shall be those involving any of the following acts, if committed against persons or property protected by the Convention: wilful killing, torture or inhuman treatment, including biological experiments, wilfully causing great suffering or serious injury to body or health, compelling a prisoner of war to serve in the forces of the hostile Power, or wilfully depriving a prisoner of war of the rights of fair and regular trial prescribed in this Convention.

[46] 46GC Article 147 states: Grave breaches to which the preceding Article relates shall be those involving any of the following acts, if committed against persons or property protected by the present Convention: wilful killing, torture or inhuman treatment, including biological experiments, wilfully causing great suffering or serious injury to body or health, unlawful deportation or transfer or unlawful confinement of a protected person, compelling a protected person to serve in the forces of a hostile Power, or wilfully depriving a protected person of the rights of fair and regular trial prescribed in the present Convention, taking of hostages and extensive destruction and appropriation of property, not justified by military necessity and carried out unlawfully and wantonly.

[47] GPW art. 4B(2) requires neutral countries to intern persons falling within the provisions of overall art. 4, that is, who would be entitled to POW status. *See* LEVIE, *supra* note 23, at 69 (noting that predecessor rule during WWII resulted in the internment of more than 100,000 POWs in neutral countries).

[48] The Protecting Power (PP) is a classic international-law device by which States engaging in armed conflict select mutually acceptable neutral nations to serve as their representatives in communicating with the other belligerent power. *See* GEOFFREY BEST, WAR AND LAW SINCE 1945 371 (reprinted 2001). Since 1950, however, PPs have been appointed in only four instances. *See id.* at 372. The ICRC generally carries out the responsibilities of the PP under the Conventions.

[49] *See* LEVIE, *supra* note 23, at 69.

Prisoners of War

The privileged status of prisoners of war grew from the concept of military necessity. Declarations of "no quarter" were forbidden because an enemy soldier who had become *hors de combat* – incapacitated due to injury, illness, surrender or capture – no longer posed a danger to combatants. Killing such persons or causing their needless suffering was considered to serve no valid military purpose, the objective being the incapacitation rather than the annihilation of enemy.[50] The privilege of being held as a prisoner of war was not extended to brigands, pirates, looters and pillagers not associated with the uniformed army of any state. Such persons were considered common criminals acting for personal gain rather than agents of a state, and they could be summarily shot.[51] (Modern rules require a fair criminal trial).[52]

The first codified set of rules for the protection of prisoners of war was General Orders 100 (known as the Lieber Code), adopted by the Union Army during the Civil War. It covered "[a]ll soldiers of whatever species of arms; all men who belong to the rising en masse of the hostile country; all those who are attached to the army for its efficiency, and promote directly the object of war..." as well as "citizens who accompany an army for whatever purpose, such as sutlers, editors, or reporters of journals, or contractors, if captured ...."[53] It was forbidden to declare that every member of a legitimate levy *en masse* – a spontaneous uprising of citizens in opposition to an armed invasion – would be treated as a bandit, but once the invading army had established itself as occupying force, citizens could not lawfully rise up against it.[54]

Later conventions adopted the Lieber Code for international application and clarified the rules, generally expanding their coverage and increasing their protections.[55] The United States Army Field Manual (FM) 27-10, The Law of Land Warfare is the main source for the Army's modern interpretation of the law of war, incorporating reference to relevant

---

[50] *See* DONALD A. WELLS, THE LAWS OF LAND WARFARE 127 (1992).
[51] *See id.*
[52] *See* Hague Convention No. IV Respecting the Laws and Customs of War on Land art. 30, Oct. 18, 1907, 36 Stat. 2277, 205 Consol. T.S. 277.
[53] *See id.* at 127-28.
[54] General Orders No. 100 para. 52.
[55] *See* PICTET, *supra* note 28, at 25 (noting Third Geneva Convention of 1949 has 143 articles plus annexes; compared with 97 in the Geneva Convention of 1929, and the chapter of the Hague Regulations on prisoners had only 17 articles). GPW art. 4 was intended to expand the coverage of the protection. *See id.* at 100.

international conventions and rules of the customary law of war, as well as relevant statutes.[56] Army Regulation (AR) 190-8 prescribes the treatment to be accorded to prisoners based on their status.[57] The U.S. military also incorporates the law of war into rules of engagement (ROE) prepared for specific combat operations,[58] providing instructions to soldiers on the lawful handling of prisoners.

The authority to detain enemy combatants continues to rest on a theory of agency or allegiance to the state. Enemy soldiers are presumed to follow the orders of commanders, therefore, if hostilities cease, soldiers can be expected to cease their fighting and will no longer pose a threat. There is thus no longer any military need to keep them in captivity under article 21 of GPW.

Civilian Detainees

Civilians in occupied territory or the territory of a belligerent may be interned during war if necessary for reasons of security.[59] The Fourth Geneva Convention (GC) protects civilians who fall into the hands of the enemy, providing protections similar to those afforded POWs under the GPW. Enemy civilians, that is, those civilians with the nationality of the opposing belligerent state, have the status of "protected person" under the GC, as long as that state is a party to the GC.[60] Nationals of a neutral or co-belligerent states who fall into the hands of a belligerent state are not entitled to the status of "protected persons" as long as the state of which they are nationals has normal diplomatic representation with the state in whose hands they are.[61] Presumably, these civilians would be protected through the diplomatic efforts of their home country and would not be exposed to the same vulnerabilities as are the citizens of the belligerent states themselves. However, Common Article 3 provides a set of minimum standards for all

---

[56] *See* Department of the Army, FM 27-10, The Law of Land Warfare, chapter 1, § 1 (1956) (listing treaties pertinent to land warfare to which the United States is a party).

[57] Department of the Army, AR 190-8, Enemy Prisoners of War, Retained Personnel, Civilian Internees and Other Detainees (1997).

[58] *See* Lt. Col. Marc L. Warren, *Operational Law – A Concept Matures*, 152 MIL. L. REV. 33, 51-57 (1996) (explaining function of ROE).

[59] GC art. 42 ("The internment or placing in assigned residence of protected persons may be ordered only if the security of the Detaining Power makes it absolutely necessary.").

[60] GC art. 4.

[61] *Id.*

persons, whether or not they are "protected persons."[62] Furthermore, part II of the GC applies universally without regard to the nationality of the civilians affected.[63]

Civilians who participate in combat, unlike combatants, are not acting on behalf of a higher authority with whom peace can be negotiated; therefore, they are not immune from punishment for belligerent acts. Their conduct is dealt with according to the law of the criminal jurisdiction in which it occurred, which could mean a civil trial or trial by a military tribunal convened by an occupying power. The GC does not state that civilians who engage in combat thereby lose their protection under the Convention. They lose their protection as civilians in the sense that they may become lawful targets for the duration of their participation in combat, but their status as civilians does not change according to the Convention. Traditionally, such a person would be regarded as an "unlawful combatant."

Unlawful Belligerents

There is no definition or separate status under the Geneva Conventions for "unlawful belligerents." However, the law of war has denied the status of privileged combatant to warriors who conduct violence for private rather than public purposes or who carry out specific unprivileged acts.[64] There are traditionally two types of unlawful belligerents: combatants who may be authorized to fight by a legitimate party to a conflict but whose perfidious conduct disqualifies them from the privileges of a POW, and civilians who are not authorized as combatants but nevertheless participate in hostilities.

Spies, Saboteurs, and Mercenaries

The first type of unlawful belligerents includes spies, saboteurs and mercenaries. These persons are acting on behalf of a state and probably under its orders, but are nonetheless denied the status of lawful belligerents.

---

[62] *See* George H. Aldrich, *The Laws of War on Land*, 94 AM. J. INT'L L. 42, 60-61 (2000) (citing international court cases for the proposition that Common Article 3 states customary international law with regard to international armed conflicts).

[63] *See* GC art. 4 (stating "[t]he provisions of Part II are, however, wider in application, as defined in Article 13").

[64] *See* Mallison and Mallison, *supra* note 19, at 42.

Spies and Saboteurs

A spy is one who, in disguise or under false pretenses, penetrates behind enemy lines of a belligerent to obtain information with the intent of communicating that information to the hostile party.[65] If captured in the act, a spy may be denied POW treatment, tried and possibly executed.[66] However, if a spy rejoins the army of the hostile party as a lawful combatant, he is no longer subject to punishment for those acts should he later fall into the hands of the enemy.[67] Saboteurs, or enemy agents who penetrate into the territory of an adversary without openly bearing arms in order to perpetrate hostile acts are subject to similar treatment.[68] If the acts are directed against civilian targets, they will likely be termed acts of terrorism.[69] Saboteurs retain the protection of the GC,[70] and are entitled to a fair and regular trial before punishment may be administered.[71] If spies and saboteurs were to retain their entitlement to POW status, belligerents could immunize those they send behind enemy lines by making them members of the armed forces, thus eliminating the inherent risk in such conduct.[72]

GC art. 5 addresses the treatment of spies and saboteurs: Where, in the territory of a Party to the conflict, the latter is satisfied that an individual protected person is definitely suspected of or engaged in activities hostile to the security of the State, such individual person shall not be entitled to claim such rights and privileges under the present Convention as would, if exercised in the favour of such individual person, be prejudicial to the security of such State.

Where in occupied territory an individual protected person is detained as a spy or saboteur, or as a person under definite suspicion of activity hostile to the security of the Occupying Power, such person shall, in those cases where absolute military security so requires, be regarded as having forfeited rights of communication under the present Convention.

---

[65] *See* Hague Convention No. IV Respecting the Laws and Customs of War on Land art. 29, Oct. 18, 1907, 36 Stat. 2277. The U.S. codification of this rule is article 106 of the UCMJ, codified at 10 U.S.C. § 904. *See* FM 27-10 §§ 75-78.
[66] *See id.* art. 30.
[67] *See id.* art. 31.
[68] *See* FM 27-10 § 81 (citing GC III art. 4).
[69] *See* Hans Peter Gasser, *Prohibition of Terrorist Acts in International Humanitarian Law*, 253 INT'L REV. RED CROSS 200 (1986), *available at* [http://www.icrc.org].
[70] *See id.* at § 73.
[71] *See* GC IV art. 5; FM 27-10 § 248.
[72] *See* LEVIE, *supra* note 23, at 37 (noting that a person suspected of being a spy or saboteur who claims POW status is entitled to a determination by a competent tribunal under GPW art. 5).

In each case, such persons shall nevertheless be treated with humanity, and in case of trial, shall not be deprived of the rights of fair and regular trial prescribed by the present Convention. They shall also be granted the full rights and privileges of a protected person under the present Convention at the earliest date consistent with the security of the State or Occupying Power, as the case may be.

Mercenaries

Mercenaries are persons who are not members of the armed forces of a party to the conflict but participate in combat for personal gain.[73] They may be authorized, or

at least encouraged to fight by a party to the conflict, but their allegiance to the authorizing party is conditioned on payment rather than obedience and loyalty.[74] It is seen as questionable whether mercenaries can serve as valid agents of a party to the conflict, or are, rather, mere "contract killers," especially considering they could just as easily switch sides to accept a better offer; may be operating in pursuit of different objectives from those of the party to the conflict; and may have an incentive for keeping the conflict live. In that sense, they are theoretically similar to brigands, looters, and bounty hunters,[75] who may take advantage of hostilities to conduct unlawful looting for their own enrichment without regard for military necessity or the law of

---

[73] *See* Protocol Additional to the Geneva Conventions of 12 August 1949, and Relating to the Protection of Victims of International Armed Conflicts (Protocol I), June 8, 1977, *reprinted in* 16 I.L.M. 1391. Art. 47 defines mercenary as follows: 2. A mercenary is any person who: (a) Is specially recruited locally or abroad in order to fight in an armed conflict; (b) Does, in fact, take a direct part in the hostilities; (c) Is motivated to take part in the hostilities essentially by the desire for private gain and, in fact, is promised, by or on behalf of a Party to the conflict, material compensation substantially in excess of that promised or paid to combatants of similar ranks and functions in the armed forces of that Party; (d) Is neither a national of a Party to the conflict nor a resident of territory controlled by a Party to the conflict; (e) Is not a member of the armed forces of a Party to the conflict; and (f) Has not been sent by a State which is not a Party to the conflict on official duty as a member of its armed forces.

[74] *See* Lieutenant Commander Gregory P. Noone, *The History and Evolution of the Law of War Prior to World War* II, 47 NAVAL L. REV. 176, 187 (2000) (recounting origin of prohibition on mercenaries after the Middle Ages).

[75] The United States has traditionally regarded the use of bounty hunters and private assassins as uncivilized. The 1914 Rules of Land Warfare stated: Civilized nations look with horror upon rewards for the assassination of enemies, the perpetrator of such an act has no claim to be treated as a combatant, but should be treated as a criminal. So, too, the proclaiming of an individual belonging to the hostile army, or a citizen or subject of the hostile government, an out-law, who may be slain without trial by a captor. The article includes not only assaults upon individuals, but as well any offer for an individual "dead or alive." *See* RULES OF LAND WARFARE para. 179 (U.S. War Department 1917).

war.[76] However, merely having a nationality other than that of the party on whose side a soldier fights does not automatically make that soldier a mercenary.[77]

It has been suggested that non-Afghan members of the Taliban and al Qaeda might be mercenaries and disqualified from POW privileges on that basis.[78] Based on press reports and Pentagon statements about the detainees, there is little to suggest that their motives stem from personal material gain rather than a belief that they are serving a higher power. It appears to be generally recognized that the fighters do not believe themselves to be serving Afghanistan as a country but are serving either the Taliban or al Qaeda, perhaps both, for ideological reasons. The United States has made it clear that it is not fighting against the Afghan people, but instead considers the Taliban and al Qaeda to be the enemies. Since both groups are considered to be parties to the conflict and their conduct serves as justification for the United States' combat operations in Afghanistan, the label of mercenary does not appear appropriate for the groups as a whole, although some of the individual fighters may prove to be mercenaries.

Civilians Who Engage in Combat

The second category of unlawful belligerents consists of civilians who carry out belligerent acts that might well be conducted lawfully by combatants with proper authorization of the state. They act on their own, albeit perhaps for patriotic or ideological reasons. Because they do not answer to any higher command, they are not valid agents of a party to the conflict and cannot always be expected to lay down their arms when hostilities between parties cease. Civilians who engage in combat lose their protected status and may become lawful targets for so long as they continue to fight. They do not enjoy immunity under the law of war for their violent conduct and can be tried and punished under civil law for their belligerent acts. However, they do not lose their protection as civilians under the GC if they are captured.

---

[76] *See* MCCOUBREY, *supra* note 35, at 145 (noting the "disturbing" role of mercenaries in the conflict in Angola as "contract killers").

[77] *See id.*(noting that not all foreigners in service of armed forces of other countries should be treated as "mercenaries," as some may serve with the approval of their home governments or for moral or ideological reasons); LEVIE, *supra* note 23, at 75 (describing entitlement to POW status of nationals of neutral states or states allied with enemy state as well-settled, while status of individual who is national of capturing state or its allies is subject to dispute).

[78] *See* Joseph Samuels, *Unconventional Prisoners*, GLOBE & MAIL (Toronto), Jan. 24, 2002, at A21 (opining that U.S. treatment of detainees is consistent with Geneva Protocols).

It would seem that the Taliban and al Qaeda do not exactly fit the second definition of unlawful combatants, either. Again, it appears they are considered to be parties to the conflict who may lawfully be treated as military targets whether or not they are directly participating in the immediate hostilities. If every Taliban or al Qaeda fighter is considered a civilian participating in an armed conflict without authorization who can be tried for ordinary acts of combat, then the question might be asked whether an armed conflict exists at all, there being no apparent legitimate force opposing the United States.[79]

Guerrillas and "Non-POWs"?

Some argue there is a third category of unlawful belligerents, comprised of all members of organized groups of irregular fighters that do not meet the criteria to be treated as prisoners of war.[80] These groups typically employ unorthodox guerrilla tactics emphasizing stealth and surprise,[81] and have received somewhat uneven treatment at the hands of states.[82] In some conflicts, irregulars who could not prove their affiliation to an official military were summarily shot as *franc-tireurs*.[83] The lack of international consensus with regard to the treatment of insurgents and partisans contributed to the international impetus to codify the law of war, but has not been resolved and remains a source of contention among states parties to the resulting treaties.[84] Guerrilla tactics do not appear to be in and of themselves violative of international law.[85] It could be argued that conventional style warfare conducted by irregular soldiers is no worse. Under this view, members of irregular armies who carry out ordinarily lawful belligerent acts,

---

[79] *See* discussion on "Characterizing the Conflict," *infra*.
[80] *See* A TREATISE ON THE JURIDICAL BASIS OF THE DISTINCTION BETWEEN LAWFUL COMBATANT AND UNPRIVILEGED BELLIGERENT 7 (U.S. Army Judge Advocate General's School 1959) (hereinafter "TREATISE") (noting the Geneva Conventions do not state that fighters who do not pass the four part test of article 4 are illegal combatants, and that therefore, if they are to be so considered, it is only because of customary international law).
[81] *See* Mallison and Mallison, *supra* note 19, at 42.
[82] *See generally* TREATISE, *supra* note 80, at 11-42 (describing varying treatment given irregulars at the hands of different states, and even by the same state during different phases of a conflict).
[83] *See id.* at 44 (citing the example of the Franco-Prussian War as impetus for advancements in the law of war allowing irregular fighters to qualify as belligerents).
[84] *See* Baxter, *supra* note 18, at 327 (arguing the 1949 Geneva Conventions destroyed what little certainty had existed in the law regarding status of irregulars).
[85] *See id.* at 337 (noting distinction between those fighting for private gain and those fighting because of genuine allegiance to a cause).

or who have not personally carried out any hostile acts, while not necessarily entitled to POW privileges, are not punishable as unlawful combatants. Like POWs, they would be subject to internment at the hands of the state without necessarily being charged with a crime. Their detention would be based on membership in the irregular army rather than citizenship and suspicion.

The issue remains: what set of rules applies to them? Some argue that, in the very least, Common Article 3 applies as well as other international human rights law. Others argue that neither peacetime civil law nor the law of war applies, essentially leaving them outside international law altogether.

Characterizing the Conflict

In order to determine the legal status of the detainees, it is first necessary to determine whether an armed conflict exists, and if so, whether that conflict is "international" or "non-international." The type of armed conflict depends upon the status of the parties to the conflict and the nature of the hostilities. The status and rights of individuals depend, in turn, on the relationship of those individuals to the parties to the conflict. It may also become important to determine the temporal and geographical boundaries of the armed conflict – for the most part, the Geneva Conventions would not apply to conduct that occurred prior to the onset or after the end of the armed conflict, nor would it apply to conduct occurring on the territory of a non-party to the conflict. Whether the territory on which the punishable conduct occurred is considered "occupied" or "partially occupied" may also be relevant to determining the status of detainees and the law applicable to them.[86]

The Geneva Conventions apply in full to "all cases of declared war or of any other armed conflict which may arise between two or more of the High Contracting Parties, even if the state of war is not recognized by one of them,"[87] or in "any cases of partial or total occupation of the territory of a High Contracting Party." Common Article 3 of the Geneva Conventions applies to internal hostilities serious enough to amount to an armed

---

[86] See GC sec. III; but see W.T. Mallison & R.A. Jabri, *The Juridical Characteristics of Belligerent Occupation and the Resort to Resistance by the Civilian Population: Doctrinal Development and Continuity*, 42 GEO. WASH. L. REV. 185, 189 (1974) (arguing that the 1949 Geneva Conventions removed the traditional distinction between "invasion" and "belligerent occupation" as far as the treatment of civilians is concerned).

[87] GPW art. 2; GC art. 2.

conflict,[88] although the parties are encouraged to adopt voluntarily the remaining provisions with respect to each other. In the case of sporadic violence involving unorganized groups and uprisings, the law of war is not implicated, although the law of basic human rights continues to apply. The classification of an armed conflict presents few difficulties in the case of a declared war between two states. Such a conflict would clearly qualify as an international armed conflict to which the Geneva Conventions would apply in their entirety. Such conflicts have also become rare. The term "internal armed conflict" generally describes a civil war taking place within the borders of a state, featuring an organized rebel force capable of controlling at least some territory. Internal conflicts may be more difficult to classify as such because states frequently deny that a series of violent acts amounts to an armed conflict.[89] Classifying a conflict in which a foreign state intervenes in an internal armed conflict creates an even more complex puzzle. Some theorists consider an armed conflict to remain internal where a foreign state intervenes on behalf of a legitimate government to put down an insurgency, whereas foreign intervention on behalf of a rebel movement would "internationalize" the armed conflict.[90] Under this view, the war in Afghanistan was an internal conflict between the Taliban and Northern

---

[88] Common Article 3 of the Geneva Conventions of 1949 states: In the case of armed conflict not of an international character occurring in the territory of one of the High Contracting Parties, each Party to the conflict shall be bound to apply, as a minimum, the following provisions: 1. Persons taking no active part in the hostilities, including members of armed forces who have laid down their arms and those placed hors de combat by sickness, wounds, detention, or any other cause, shall in all circumstances be treated humanely, without any adverse distinction founded on race, colour, religion or faith, sex, birth or wealth, or any other similar criteria. To this end, the following acts are and shall remain prohibited at any time and in any place whatsoever with respect to the above-mentioned persons: (a) Violence to life and person, in particular murder of all kinds, mutilation, cruel treatment and torture; (b) Taking of hostages; (c) Outrages upon personal dignity, in particular humiliating and degrading treatment; (d) The passing of sentences and the carrying out of executions without previous judgment pronounced by a regularly constituted court, affording all the judicial guarantees which are recognized as indispensable by civilized peoples. 2. The wounded and sick shall be collected and cared for. An impartial humanitarian body, such as the International Committee of the Red Cross, may offer its services to the Parties to the conflict. The Parties to the conflict should further endeavour to bring into force, by means of special agreements, all or part of the other provisions of the present Convention. The application of the preceding provisions shall not affect the legal status of the Parties to the conflict.

[89] *See* HANDBOOK, *supra* note 39, at 23.

[90] *See* John Embry Parkerson, Jr., *United States Compliance with Humanitarian Law Respecting Civilians During Operation Just Cause*, 133 MIL. L. REV. 31, 41-42 (1991) (applying analysis to determine whether U.S. invasion of Panama on behalf of Endara government made conflict "international" for the purposes of GPW).

Alliance troops until U.S. forces intervened, at which point the conflict became international.[91] When the Taliban ceded control of the government, the conflict may have reverted to an internal conflict, because U.S. forces then became aligned with the government of the state. Others view virtually any hostilities causing international repercussions to be international for the purposes of the Geneva Conventions.[92]

According to the official commentary of the International Committee of the Red Cross (ICRC),[93] the conditions for an international war are satisfied whenever any difference arises leading to the use of armed force between the militaries of two states.[94] Both the United States and Afghanistan are signatories to the four Geneva Conventions of 1949. If the Taliban was, at the onset of the conflict, the government of Afghanistan and its soldiers were the regular armed forces, it would appear that the present conflict meets the Geneva Conventions' definition of an international armed conflict. However, only three states ever recognized the Taliban as the legitimate government of Afghanistan. While it is not necessary for the governments of states engaging in hostilities to recognize each other,[95] the rules are less clear where virtually no country recognizes a government.

Because the use of force by private persons rather than organs of a state has not traditionally constituted an "act of war,"[96] it is arguable that refusing to recognize the Taliban as a *de facto* government of a state would preclude the United States from prosecuting the September 11 terrorist attacks as "war crimes." After all, it has been suggested that international terrorism might be considered to amount to armed conflict for the purposes of the law of war only if a foreign government is involved.[97]

---

[91] *See* Do the Laws of War Apply to the War on Terror?, Public Meeting of the American Society of International Law, Feb. 13, 2002 (hereinafter ASIL Meeting) (comments of Prof. Robert Goldman) (audio *available at* [http://www.sais-jhu.edu/mediastream/intlaw.ram]).

[92] *See* Maj. Geoffrey S. Corn and Maj. Michael Smidt, "*To Be or Not to Be, That is the Question": Contemporary Military Operations and the Status of Captured Personnel,* ARMY LAW. June 1999 (citing interview with DoD law of war expert Hayes Parks, who advocates a purely *de facto* standard, without regard to political factors).

[93] *See* INTERNATIONAL COMMITTEE OF THE RED CROSS, COMMENTARY ON THE GENEVA CONVENTIONS, (J. Pictet, ed., 1960) (hereinafter "ICRC Commentary"). The ICRC was instrumental in drafting the Geneva Conventions and continues to act as a "custodian" of international humanitarian law.

[94] *See id.* at 23.

[95] GPW art. 4A(3).

[96] HANDBOOK, *supra* note 39, at 42.

[97] *See* LT. COL. RICHARD J. ERICKSON, LEGITIMATE USE OF MILITARY FORCE AGAINST STATE- SPONSORED INTERNATIONAL TERRORISM 66-67 (1989) (arguing that state sponsored or state supported terrorist organizations may have status

The level of state support of terrorism required to incur state responsibility under international law is a matter of debate.[98] Denying that *any* state is involved in the terrorist acts that precipitated the armed conflict could call into question the United States' treatment of those attacks as violations of the law of war.

Some observers cite additional policy grounds for treating the armed conflict as international. To treat it as an internal conflict could have implications for U.S. and allied troops. *No one* would be entitled to POW status or "protected person" status under the third and fourth Geneva Conventions, although Common Article 3 would remain in force for all parties. U.S. and coalition soldiers may be placed at risk of capture in Afghanistan or elsewhere depending on how the conflict proceeds. The President's recent decision to apply the Geneva Conventions to the Taliban but deny their application to al Qaeda as a non-party may be an implicit recognition that the armed conflict is an international one.

Interpretation of GPW Article 4

Assuming the conflict is international, both the United States and Afghanistan, as signatories to the four Geneva Conventions of 1949, are bound to grant POW status to enemy combatants who qualify under GPW article 4. Members of the armed forces, including militias and volunteer corps serving as part of the armed forces, who are captured are entitled to be treated as POWs. Members of other volunteer corps, militias, and organized resistance forces belonging to a party to the conflict are entitled to POW status only if the organization meets the four criteria in GPW article 4A(2). The regular armed forces of a state,[99] even if it is a government or "authority" not recognized by the opposing party,[100] need not necessarily satisfy the four criteria in order for their members to be entitled to POW status under the GPW art. 4A(2). However, members of regular armed forces

---

under international law, while terrorist organizations not recognized as international entities might best be dealt with as criminal matters).

[98] *See* Gregory M. Travalio, *Terrorism, International Law, and the Use of Military Force*, 18 WIS. INT'L L.J. 145, 148 (2000) (citing General Assembly Resolutions 2131 that states have a "duty to refrain from organizing, instigating, assisting, or participating in acts of civil strife or terrorist acts in another state or acquiescing in organized activities within its territory....").

[99] GPW art. 4A(1).

[100] GPW art. 4A(3).

may be denied POW rights if they are caught as spies or saboteurs behind enemy lines.[101] Under this view, Taliban soldiers captured on the battlefield in Afghanistan are at least presumptively lawful combatants entitled to POW status.

Al Qaeda is not claimed as the armed forces of Afghanistan; therefore, its members are entitled to POW status only if it "forms part of" the armed forces of Afghanistan, it "belongs to" the Taliban and meets the four criteria in GPW art. 4A(2), or it can be considered "an authority" not recognized by the United States but nevertheless a party to the conflict.

GPW Art. 4A(1): Does al Qaeda Form "part of" the Armed Forces of a Party to the Conflict?

The GPW provides little guidance for making the determination whether an armed militia or volunteer group "forms part of" the regular army of a party to a conflict for the purposes of article 4A(1). The determination may be made in accordance with the national laws of the state party to the conflict.[102] The language may have been included in order to ensure that members of the United States National Guard, for example, are protected.[103] However, in the case of states with less developed military organizations, including newly emerging states or new governments, the determination may not be as clear. If some al Qaeda combat units are officially incorporated into the Taliban army, members of those units could argue that they are entitled to POW status.[104]

---

[101] See LEVIE, *supra* note 23, at 36-37 (explaining that a soldier wearing civilian clothes captured in enemy territory engaged in sabotage or espionage is no more entitled to POW treatment than a civilian in the same situation, lest states incorporate saboteurs and spies into their armed forces to immunize them for violations of the law of war).

[102] See *id.* at 36 (noting, however, that states may not use domestic legislation to bring otherwise unlawful combatants under the protection of the GPW).

[103] See LEVIE, *supra* note 23, at 38.

[104] See Douglas Cassel, *Case by Case: What Defines a POW?*, CHI. TRIB., Feb. 3, 2002 (noting that at least one al Qaeda battalion is reportedly incorporated into the Taliban armed forces, possibly entitling those soldiers to POW status upon capture).

GPW Art. 4A(2): Does al Qaeda "belong to" a Party to the Conflict?

Even if al Qaeda is not part of the armed forces of Afghanistan, its members could qualify as POWs if al Qaeda "belongs to" a party to the conflict and it meets the criteria under GPW art. 4A(2). Presumably, "belonging to" a party would be a less exacting standard than "forming part of" its armed forces. It may be that informal and even temporary cooperation between the militia or volunteer group and regular troops suffices to bring militia members under the protection of combatant status.[105] The inclusion of the phrase "organized resistance groups" complicates the interpretation. The phrase was apparently included to address resistance movements of the type that sprang up in many occupied territories during World War II.[106] If a militia is fighting on behalf of a government-in-exile, the question arises as to whether that government is still a party to the conflict to which a resistance group might validly belong.[107]

If no party to the conflict claims a partisan group or authorizes it to engage in combat, there may be insufficient proof that the group is covered. An Israeli court confronted the question when members of the Popular Front for the Liberation of Palestine (PLFP) sought to overturn criminal convictions for acts they committed in the West Bank by claiming POW status.[108] The court upheld the civil convictions, holding that since no government with which Israel was then at war claimed responsibility for the actions of the PLFP, its members were not entitled to be treated as POWs. Because the occupied territory of the West Bank previously belonged to Jordan, a signatory of the GPW, the PLFP could only belong to "a party" if it belonged to Jordan. Since the group was illegal in Jordan, the court reasoned its members were not protected as POWs.[109]

---

[105] See Mallison and Mallison, *supra* note 19, at 52 (suggesting "belonging" element could be satisfied by mere *de facto* relationship between the irregular unit and a state).

[106] See Cassel, *supra* note 104, at 40, n.151 (distinguishing resistance movement in international conflict from rebel groups in civil wars for the purpose of article 4).

[107] See *id.* at 41 (concluding that indigenous groups resisting invading forces are likely meant to be covered, but recognizing ambiguity with respect to groups supporting the invading army).

[108] Military Prosecutor v. Kassem, 47 I.L.R. 470 (1971) (excerpts reprinted in DOCUMENTS ON PRISONERS OF WAR, document no. 160 (U.S. Naval War College 1979) (hereinafter "POW DOCUMENTS").

[109] *But see* Mallison and Mallison, *supra* note 19, at 71-72 (arguing status of PFLP under Jordanian law was not relevant to the question of whether it "belonged to" a party).

On the other hand, governments are not always willing to acknowledge their support of irregular armed groups, meaning a partisan group may have to establish a *de facto* relationship through other means.[110] United States officials have argued that the Taliban and al Qaeda are intimately connected.[111] That connection is arguably what makes the Taliban responsible for the terrorist acts of al Qaeda. For that reason, it may be counterproductive for United States Officials to take the position that al Qaeda does not belong to the Taliban for the purposes of applying GPW art. 4.

The Four Criteria

The four criteria in GPW art. 4A(2) appear to be at the center of the debate about the POW status of detainees. The main issue is whether the four criteria apply only to irregulars, as the text and structure of the treaty suggests, or whether they form a part of customary international law and apply to *all* combatants.[112] Unfortunately, there is not much legal precedent that can serve as a very helpful aid in interpreting and applying the criteria.[113]

The four criteria have their roots in the earliest expressions of the laws of war, beginning with the Brussels Declaration[114] and continuing nearly

---

[110] *See* LEVIE, *supra* note 23, at 42 (citing GPW commentary suggesting that supply of arms might be evidence of relationship).

[111] *See* Press Conference, Department of Defense, Secretary Rumsfeld Media Availability en route to Camp X-Ray, Jan. 27, 2002, *a v a i l a b l e a t* [http://www.defenselink.mil/news /Jan2002/ t01282002_t0127sd2.html]. With respect to the Taliban, the Taliban also did not wear uniforms, they did not have insignia, they did not carry their weapons openly, and they were tied tightly at the waist to al Qaeda. They behaved like them, they worked with them, they functioned with them, they cooperated with respect to communications, they cooperated with respect to supplies and ammunition, and there isn't any question in my mind – I'm not a lawyer, but there isn't any question in my mind but that they are not, they would not rise to the standard of a prisoner of war.

[112] *See* LEVIE, *supra* note 23, at 36 -37 (commenting that the lack of criteria under article 4A(1) "does not mean that mere membership in the regular armed forces will automatically entitle an individual who is captured to [POW] status if his conduct prior to and at the time of capture have not met these requirements."). However, the examples he lists have to do with individual spies and saboteurs, that is, individual soldiers who pose as civilians to conduct hostile activities behind enemy lines. It is arguably a different matter to apply the standards to regular armies as a whole.

[113] *See* TREATISE, *supra* note 80, at 86-87 (predicting nations would be unlikely to adopt definitions that might foreclose future options, and noting that prior practice was relatively useless as precedent, consisting of a "collection of varying and conflicting policy decisions made on an ad hoc basis").

[114] *See* LEVIE, *supra* note 23, at 44 (noting that Declaration of Brussels, based largely on the Lieber Code, never entered into force but served as a source for later conventions).

unchanged in the Hague Convention Respecting the Laws and Customs of War on Land of 1907,[115] and are repeated in the GPW. However, this may be more a reflection of nations' inability to agree on a better formula than an indication of the solidity of their foundation.[116] The criteria may reflect the customs of war as they existed among the European countries who signed the original treaties, but were not viewed at the time as universal.[117] The criteria originated as a compromise between states with strong standing armies and weaker states whose defense might depend on armed citizens.[118] The only real effect of the enumeration of the criteria at the Hague was to prohibit ill treatment of those who do not meet them.[119]

Historically, the most important consideration given to POW status has been whether there is evidence that they serve a government or political entity that exercises authority over them.[120] For example, the United States practice as early as 1900, during the Philippine Insurrection following the Spanish-American War, was to accord prisoner of war status to members of the insurgent army recognized by the Philippine government who complied "in general" with the four conditions.[121] Members of guerrilla bands not part of the regular forces were punished severely for acts of violence. A similar policy was adopted by the British during the South African War, although the first inclination was to declare that, inasmuch as the newly annexed Orange River Colony was British territory, inhabitants who took up arms

---

[115] Hague Convention No. IV Respecting the Laws and Customs of War on Land, Oct. 18, 1907, 36 Stat. 2277, 205 Consol. T.S. 277. Article 1 states: The laws, rights, and duties of war apply not only to armies, but also to militia and volunteer corps, fulfilling the following conditions: To be commanded by a person responsible for his subordinates; To have a fixed distinctive emblem recognizable at a distance; To carry arms openly; and To conduct their operations in accordance with the laws and customs of war. In countries where militia or volunteer corps constitute the army, or form part of it, they are included under the denomination "army."

[116] See TREATISE, *supra* note 80, at 48 (attributing the reluctance to adopt any change in the criteria to the sensitivity of the subject).

[117] See id. at 95 (pointing out that the reasons for defining irregulars as such are the product of "western minds," and that the "gulf between the occidental and oriental concept of war is vast").

[118] See id. at 7 (noting that the "four criteria, being the product of a compromise of violently conflicting interests, are vague and open to varying interpretations").

[119] See id. at 52 (noting that the Hague Convention did not enact any new positive law, but only attempted to codify the existing rules and prohibit certain acts).

[120] See generally, Lester Nurich and Roger W. Barret, *Legality of Guerrilla Forces under the Laws of War*, 40 AM. J. INT'L L 563 (1946) (surveying history of armed conflict from 1847 through the Second World War).

[121] See id. at 576 (describing official statements as well as practice with regard to different types of guerrillas).

were to be treated as rebels.[122] Foreign jurists and some prominent British statesman objected to the policy as a "monstrous proclamation ... absolutely opposed to the first principles of international law and history."[123] A new proclamation was issued to declare that only those inhabitants who had not been a continuous part of the fighting would be treated as rebels. British forces punished as "marauders" those who carried out acts of hostility who did not belong to "an organized body authorized by a recognized Government."[124]

On the other hand, toward the end of the Mexican War, in 1847, United States forces changed from a more tolerant policy toward irregulars to one of utmost severity. By that time, warfare by bands of guerrillas sanctioned by the late Mexican government had become the primary means of resistance. Once the war degenerated to the point where the guerrillas more resembled murderers and highway robbers than soldiers, the U.S. Secretary of War directed General Winfield Scott to adopt a policy of less forbearance than had hitherto been observed.[125] In 1870, during the Franco- Prussian War, the German commanders refused to treat any irregular fighters as lawful combatants, even those who possessed papers proving their affiliation with the government.[126]

It was a fundamental part of the law of war that only combatants authorized to fight on behalf of a state party to a conflict were allowed to participate in the hostilities. It has never been permitted to wage war against civilians.[127] Civilians could become lawful military objectives only if and for so long as they took up arms against a belligerent. The four criteria are meant to ensure that only persons authorized to fight on behalf of a higher authority who is responsible for their conduct will participate, excluding civilians as both combatants and targets.

Supporters of granting POW status to Taliban soldiers argue that the text of the Conventions should be read literally. That the four criteria are listed only under the sub-paragraph for volunteer groups and militias not forming part of the regular army of a state indicates that there is no similar test for those whose status as members of a state military force is not in doubt. Others, however, argue that regular soldiers must already meet those criteria under international law, and the drafters of the GPW felt it would be

---

[122] *See id.* at 578.
[123] *See id.* (citing statemnt by James Bryce in the House of Commons).
[124] *See id.* at 579.
[125] *See id.* at 579.
[126] *See id.* at 573.
[127] *See* WILLIAM WINTHROP, MILITARY LAW AND PRECEDENTS 778 (2d. ed. 2000).

superfluous to list the criteria with regard to regular armies. Article 1 of the 1907 Hague Convention could be read to apply the four criteria to all military forces. However, inasmuch as that article states that not only the rights, but the laws and duties of war as well, apply only to the parties it lists, such an interpretation could lead to the conclusion that regular armies could evade their obligations under the law of war by not fulfilling the four conditions.

(a) Commanded by a Person Responsible for his Subordinates

According to U.S. military doctrine, the responsible command element is fulfilled if:

> the commander of the corps is a commissioned officer of the armed forces or is a person of position and authority or if the members of the militia or volunteer corps are provided with documents, badges, or other means of identification to show that they are officers, noncommissioned officers, or soldiers so that there may be no doubt that they are not persons acting on their own responsibility. State recognition, however, is not essential, and an organization may be formed spontaneously and elect its own officers.[128]

The key to the first element is that the subject is acting on behalf of and on the command of a higher authority. The Secretary of Defense has suggested that the Taliban do not fulfill this requirement because "they were not organized in military units, as such, with identifiable chains of command; indeed, al Qaeda forces made up portions of their forces."[129] However, in response to a reporter who asked whether it was not clear that the Taliban were operating as a cohesive unit, pointing to previous reports that the U.S. military had successfully attacked "command and control" elements, Secretary Rumsfeld responded that while such a case could be made for the first (command) element, it would be difficult to argue the Taliban meet all four criteria, suggesting that that element may not be critical to the Administration's position.

A possible drawback to setting a high standard of conventional military organization to determine whether the Taliban or al Qaeda meet the "responsible command" element is that it could contradict the justification for targeting them at all. If there is insufficient command and control of the forces to distinguish the Taliban from a lawless mob, it would be unlikely that those forces would pose a significant threat, especially outside of

---

[128] FM 27-10 para. 64a.
[129] *See* Rumsfeld Press Conference, *supra* note 3.

Afghanistan. If there is no central authority directing the conduct of the fighters, they would be considered mere civilians whose targeting would accomplish little toward the objective of conquering the foe. It also raises a question as to the possible value of any intelligence to be gained through interrogating them.

(b) Uses a Fixed Distinctive Sign Recognizable at a Distance
According to FM 27-10,

> the requirement for a "fixed distinctive sign" is satisfied: by the wearing of military uniform, but less than the complete uniform will suffice. A helmet or headdress which would make the silhouette of the individual readily distinguishable from that of an ordinary civilian would satisfy this requirement. It is also desirable that the individual member of the militia or volunteer corps wear a badge or brassard permanently affixed to his clothing. It is not necessary to inform the enemy of the distinctive sign, although it may be desirable to do so in order to avoid misunderstanding.[130]

The GPW does not clarify what is meant by "fixed" or by "distinctive," despite the fact that the same language gave rise to disputes as it was interpreted in earlier treaties.[131] Presumably, the requirement for a sign to be "fixed" was meant to prevent fighters from removing them easily, but it is unlikely the requirement was meant to remain in force even when no military operations were ongoing.[132] Similarly, there is nothing to explain how great a distance must be before the distinction need no longer be discernible. Methods of locating and of camouflaging military targets, including soldiers, make it questionable whether the standards are the same today as they were when the original Conventions were drafted, if such standards ever existed.

The purpose for requiring combatants to distinguish themselves from civilians is to protect civilians from being targeted. Combatants who are unable to distinguish enemy combatants from civilians might resort to firing upon all human beings in the area of operations. There may be other reasons for enforcing the obligation to identify oneself as a combatant that serve tactical purposes rather than purely humanitarian ends. Requiring irregulars to display a mark aids the opposing army in targeting them and also impedes the irregulars' ability to effect a surprise attack.[133] The use of different

---

[130] FM 27-10 para. 64b.
[131] See LEVIE, *supra* note 23, at 47.
[132] See Mallison and Mallison, *supra* note 19, at 56-57 (noting that armbands, insignia, or distinctive headgear are acceptable according to some military manuals).
[133] See TREATISE, *supra* note 80, at 31.

uniforms to distinguish the forces also helps leaders identify their own troops during combat, and to distinguish friendly from enemy soldiers.[134] It has also been suggested that the requirement to wear a uniform is a remnant of long outdated forms of warfare, in which closely ranked armies opposed each other across open fields.[135] Modern army uniforms are designed to make the wearer difficult to distinguish from the surrounding foliage from any distance. It has been pointed out that the requirement for irregulars is not more stringent than the standard set by regular armies.[136]

Although the lack of uniform can be detrimental to a soldier who falls into the hands of the enemy,[137] it has not been the case historically that all fighters lacking a uniform or some other identifying mark have been denied prisoner status.[138] According to FM 27-10, the lack of uniform brings the following result:

> Members of the armed forces of a party to the conflict and members of militias or volunteer corps forming part of such armed forces lose their right to be treated as prisoners of war *whenever they deliberately conceal their status in order to pass behind the military lines of the enemy for the purpose of gathering military information or for the purpose of waging war by destruction of life or property*. Putting on civilian clothes or the uniform of the enemy are examples of concealment of the status of a member of the armed forces.[139]

For a combatant to engage in hostilities while disguising his identity in order to deceive the enemy thus could amount to perfidious conduct in violation of the law of war.[140] Guerrillas and terrorists therefore lose their

---

[134] *See id.* at 76 (noting that uniforms performed a purely utilitarian function prior to the Franco-Prussian War).

[135] *See* Baxter, *supra* note 18, at 343.

[136] *See* Mallison and Mallison, *supra* note 19, at 57.

[137] *See* Baxter, *supra* note 18, at 343. ("[T]he character of the clothing worn by the accused has assumed major importance.").

[138] *See generally* TREATISE, *supra* note 80. For example, during the French and Indian War, both sides employed some irregulars, who did not wear uniforms, and these were apparently regarded as lawful combatants. *Id.* at 18-19. During the American Revolution, the British army treated colonial irregulars belonging to militias as lawful combatants despite their lack of uniforms, although individual snipers unattached to any American forces were sometimes executed. *Id.* at 20-21. In the Spanish Peninsular War (1807-1814), the French treated all irregulars as illegal combatants, even those that met the four conditions embodied in later treaties. *See id.* at 23-23.

[139] FM 27-10, *supra* note 56, at para. 74 (emphasis added.)

[140] Perfidious conduct refers to an act that "invite[s] the confidence of an adversary to lead him to believe that he is entitled to receive, or is obliged to accord protection under the rules of

claim to protected status if they place the civilian populace at risk. However, a soldier not engaging in hostilities probably has not committed a violation by using civilian disguise merely to evade detection by the enemy.[141] Soldiers who belong to armies that do not wear full uniforms are not necessarily engaging in perfidious conduct as long as they bear arms openly and do not hide their belligerent status.[142]

Secretary of Defense Rumsfeld has suggested that the Taliban do not fulfill the requirement because they "did not wear distinctive signs, insignias, symbols or uniforms. To the contrary, far from seeking to distinguish themselves from the civilian population of Afghanistan, they sought to blend in with civilian noncombatants, hiding in mosques and populated areas."[143] Critics of the Defense Department's position point out that neither the Taliban nor the Northern Alliance had ever worn uniforms or any distinctive sign, other than the black turban worn by members of the Taliban. The failure to wear what Western commanders might regard as proper military dress may be more a matter of custom than perfidy. Since most of the hand-to-hand combat was conducted by the Northern Alliance, with U.S. forces supplying intelligence and fire support from the air or at a great distance, the critics argue, the Pentagon's position that the lack of uniforms makes "unlawful combatants" of the Taliban force is less persuasive. The very success of the armed forces in quickly routing the enemy with virtually no U.S. casualties may make the argument somewhat more difficult to sustain. Finally, critics have pointed out that U.S. Special Forces troops have been known to operate occasionally in civilian dress, or even to use the uniform of the enemy for the purpose of infiltrating enemy territory.[144]

---

international law applicable in armed conflict, with intent to betray that confidence...." *See* BASIC RULES OF THE GENEVA CONVENTIONS AND THEIR ADDITIONAL PROTOCOLS 24 (ICRC ed. 1983).

[141] *See* Baxter, *supra* note 18, at 340-41 (noting probable distinction between hostile intent and seeking to escape).

[142] *See, e.g.* TREATISE, *supra* note 80, at 55-59 (describing the very unconventional commandos of the Boer Republic, which Britain treated as lawful combatants despite the fact that they wore civilian clothing and employed guerrilla tactics in the latter phase of the Boer War).

[143] *See* Rumsfeld Press Conference, *supra* note 3.

[144] *See* Gary L. Walsh, *Role of the Judge Advocate in Special Operations*, 1989-AUG ARMY LAW. 4, 6-7 (noting that while use of the enemy uniform during battle is forbidden by the law of war, U.S. policy allows use of the enemy uniform for infiltration of enemy lines).

(c) Carries Arms Openly

The requirement of carrying arms openly serves a similar purpose to that of the fixed distinctive sign, to prevent perfidious conduct in violation of the law of war. FM 27-10 describes this requirement in the negative. It is:

> not satisfied by the carrying of weapons concealed about the person or if the individuals hide their weapons on the approach of the enemy.

The ICRC notes the distinction between "carrying arms 'openly' and carrying them 'visibly' or 'ostensibly,'" stating the provision "is intended to guarantee the loyalty of the fighting (sic), it is not an attempt to prescribe that a hand-grenade or a revolver must be carried at belt or shoulder rather than in a pocket or under a coat."[145] The paramount concern "is that the enemy must be able to recognize partisans as combatants in the same way as members of regular armed forces, whatever their weapons."[146]

One question is whether arms must be carried in the open at all times or only during the conduct of actual hostilities. Since surprise attacks are not *per se* unlawful, it seems that ordinary ruses of war that involve camouflage or concealing of arms to hide preparation for battle would be permissible, while perfidious attacks carried out with weapons disguised as harmless equipment might not be allowed.

It may also be valid to question whether the requirement is the same during offensive operations for both the attacker and the attacked. To impose the same requirements on those who suddenly find themselves in battle, denying POW status on the basis that a particular combatant had a weapon concealed somewhere or was not at the time in uniform would seem to give the attacker a clear advantage and even greater incentive to launch surprise attacks against an unprepared enemy.

(d) *Conducts its Operations in Accordance with the Laws of War*

According to FM 27-10:

> This condition is fulfilled if most of the members of the body observe the laws and customs of war, notwithstanding the fact that the individual member concerned may have committed a war crime. Members of militias and volunteer corps should be especially warned against employment of treachery, denial of quarters, maltreatment of prisoners of war, wounded,

---

[145] *See* ICRC COMMENTARY, *supra* note 93, at 61.
[146] See id.

and dead, improper conduct toward flags of truce, pillage, and unnecessary violence and destruction.

The ICRC interprets the condition similarly:

> Partisans are ... required to respect the Geneva Conventions to the fullest extent possible. In particular, they must conform to international agreements such as those which prohibit the use of certain weapons (gas). In all their operations, they must be guided by the moral criteria which, in the absence of written provisions, must direct the conscience of man; in launching attacks, they must not cause violence and suffering disproportionate to the military result which they may reasonably hope to achieve. They may not attack civilians or disarmed persons and must, in all their operations, respect the principles of honour and loyalty as they expect their enemies to do.[147]

The condition is said to be vital to the recognition of irregular fighters, because states cannot be expected to adhere to the law of war to fight an enemy that is not likewise bound. However, the somewhat lenient stance just quoted reflects the fact that the "concept of the laws and customs of war is rather vague and subject to variation as the forms of war evolve."[148] The imprecision of the condition could lead to its abuse; a relatively minor violation of the law of war could be used as a pretext to deny POW status to an entire army, which would arguably give the members of an irregular army little incentive to follow *any* of the rules if adherence to a particular rule is outside their capability. [149]

One of the unresolved issues, then, is whether the criteria apply to each soldier as an individual or to the army as a whole. In other words, does the violation of a rule by one soldier result in the failure to qualify for POW status for the rest of the group, even though some members might scrupulously follow all of the rules? Can individual soldiers still qualify for POW status even though their leaders do not strictly enforce the rules over all subordinates? A member of a regular force does not lose his right to be treated as a POW by violating the law of war, so it might seem inconsistent to give members of irregular groups who might otherwise qualify harsher treatment. However, a capturing power is probably inclined to insist that

---

[147] See id.
[148] See id.
[149] *See* Mallison and Mallison, *supra* note 19, at 60 (suggesting that "it is better to have irregulars adhere as much as possible rather than not at all").

each individual detainee meet all four conditions before receiving treatment as a POW.[150]

With regard to whether a regular army forfeits the right to have its members treated as POWs by failing to follow the laws of war, U.S. practice has been to comply with the Conventions even when the opposing side of a conflict does not. The United States treated North Korean and Chinese prisoners as POWs during the armed conflict in Korea, despite the near total disregard of its provisions on the part of the Communists.[151] The United States also treated North Vietnamese and some Vietcong prisoners as POWs, despite North Vietnam's denial that the GPW applied at all,[152] along with its threatened policy of treating downed U.S. airmen as war criminals not eligible for POW status.

Determining Status under GPW Art. 5

Article 5 of GPW states: "Should any doubt arise as to whether persons, having committed a belligerent act and having fallen into the hands of the enemy," belong to any of the categories in article 4 for POWs, "such persons shall enjoy the protection of the present Convention until such time as their status has been determined by a competent tribunal." President Bush has declared with respect to the detainees that there is no ambiguity: they are "unlawful combatants" and are not entitled to POW status. Some critics argue that while most of the detainees may fail to meet the criteria for POW status, a declaration by the executive to that effect does not equate to a decision by a "competent tribunal."

The GPW does not indicate how an article 5 tribunal should be constituted or in whose mind the doubt must arise in order to compel the institution of such a tribunal. The provision is new to the 1949 GPW and was

---

[150] *See* LEVIE, *supra* note 23, at 44-45, emphasizing that: [M]ost Capturing Powers will deny the benefits and safeguards of the Convention to any such individual who is in any manner delinquent in compliance. It must also be emphasized that if an individual is found to have failed to meet the four conditions, this may make him an unprivileged combatant but it does not place him at the complete mercy of his captor, to do with as the captor arbitrarily determines. He is still entitled to the general protection of the law of war, which means that he may not be subjected to inhuman treatment, such as torture, and he is entitled to be tried before penal sanctions are imposed.

[151] *See* LEVIE, *supra* note 23, at 30 (noting that none of the parties had yet acceded to the treaties but all had agreed to be bound by their humanitarian principles).

[152] *See id.*

inserted at the request of the ICRC.[153] Prior to the inclusion of this language, summary decisions were often made by soldiers of relatively low rank on the battlefield, leading to instances where a captive could be presumed unlawful and executed on the spot, with any investigation to follow.[154] Under the 1949 GPW, combatants are presumed to be entitled to POW status unless formally declared otherwise.[155] The United States has in the past interpreted this language as requiring an individual assessment of status before privileges can be denied.[156] Any individual who claims POW status is entitled to an adjudication of that status. An individual who has not committed a belligerent act and thus claims to be an innocent civilian arguably has the right to have that claim adjudicated.

The conflict in Vietnam, with its high frequency of irregular warfare, brought about the first implementation of written procedures for art. 5 tribunals.[157] The United States Military Assistance Command (MACV) first issued a directive pertaining to the determination of POW status in 1966.[158] Under the MACV directive, the captured North Vietnamese Army and Vietcong fighters were accorded POW status upon capture.[159] "Irregulars" were divided into three groups: guerrillas, self-defense force, and secret self-defense force. Members of these groups could qualify for POW status if captured in regular combat, but were denied such status if caught in an act of "terrorism, sabotage or spying."[160] Those not treated as POWs were treated as civil defendants, and were accorded the substantive and procedural protections of the GC.[161] This approach met with the approval of the ICRC.[162]

---

[153] *See* ICRC COMMENTARY, *supra* note 93, at 77.

[154] *See* LEVIE, *supra* note 23, at 56.

[155] *See* Baxter, *supra* note 18, at 343-44 ("The judicial determination which is necessary before a person may be treated as an unprivileged belligerent is in consequence not a determination of guilt but of status only and, for the purposes of international law, it is sufficient to ascertain whether the conduct of individual has been such as to deny him the status of the prisoner or of the peaceful civilian.").

[156] *See id;* FM 27-10 para. 71 ("[Article 5] applies to any person not appearing to be entitled to prisoner-of-war status who has committed a belligerent act or has engaged in hostile activities in aid of the armed forces and who asserts that he is entitled to treatment as a prisoner of war or concerning whom any other doubt of a like nature exists.").

[157] *See* POW DOCUMENTS, *supra* note 108, at 722.

[158] See MACV Directive 20-5, 17 May 1966.

[159] *See* MACV Directive 381-46, Dec. 27, 1967 annex A, *reprinted in* 62 AM. J. INT'L L 765 (1968).

[160] *Id.*

[161] *See* Mallison and Mallison, *supra* note 19, at 73.

[162] *See id.* at 74 (quoting commendation by ICRC representative in Saigon).

The current procedures for determining the status of detainees is prescribed in United States Army Regulation (AR) 190-8. The regulation divides persons captured on the battlefield into four groups: enemy prisoners of war (EPW), retained personnel (RP - medical personnel, chaplains, and Red Cross representatives), civilian internees (CI), and other detainees (OD - whose status has not yet been determined but who are to be treated as EPW in the meantime). Ordinarily, a preliminary determination of each captive's status would be made by military police with the assistance of military intelligence personnel and interpreters during the processing procedure at the battlefield division collection point.[163] Where a captive's status cannot be adequately determined, the captive will be temporarily assigned the designation of "OD" until a tribunal can be convened to make a final determination. In the meantime, the OD is kept with the EPWs and accorded the same treatment.

AR 190-8 sec.1-6 prescribes the procedures for determining whether persons who have committed belligerent acts or engaged in hostile activities in aid of enemy armed forces are entitled to POW status, when such status is in doubt, in accordance with GPW art. 5. A tribunal composed of three commissioned officers established by a general courts-martial convening authority holds an open (to the extent allowed by security concerns) proceeding to decide by majority vote on the preponderance of evidence whether the detainee is an EPW, RP, innocent civilian, or civilian who "for reasons of operational security, or probable cause incident to criminal investigation, should be detained." It is unclear whether there are any specific time limits for a final determination. The regulation states that

> [p]ersons who have been determined by a competent tribunal not to be entitled to prisoner of war status may not be executed, imprisoned, or otherwise penalized without further proceedings to determine what acts they have committed and what penalty should be imposed.[164]

These procedures do not appear to apply in what the Army calls Military Operations Other than War (MOOTW).[165] In U.S. operations in Somalia and Haiti, for example, captured persons were termed "detainees" and were

---

[163] *See* FM 3-19.40 Military Police Internment/Resettlement (I/R) Operations.

[164] AR 190-8 ch. 1-6(g).

[165] *See* Warren, *supra* note 58, at 58 (noting that during MOOTW in Panama, Somalia, and Haiti, captured belligerents were not entitled to POW status because none was involved in an international armed conflict or captured in occupied territory). A court later ruled that the engagement in Panama amounted to an international armed conflict. *See* United States v. Noriega, 808 F.Supp.791 (S.D.Fla. 1992).

treated "in accordance with the humanitarian, but not administrative or technical standards of the GPW."[166] Human rights advocates reportedly found the living conditions acceptable, but criticized the uncertain nature of the detention. None of the detainees was ever tried by military commission as unlawful combatants.[167]

During Operation Just Cause in Panama, members of the Panamanian armed forces were termed "detainees" but were reportedly treated as POWs.[168] General Manuel Noriega, taken prisoner during the operation and removed to the United States for trial on drug charges, eventually succeeded in having a court accord him recognition as a POW.[169] The court did not agree with the Administration that since Gen. Noriega was being treated as a POW, there was no need to decide whether he was entitled to that status under international law.[170] The court stated:

> The government's position provides no assurances that the government will not at some point in the future decide that Noriega is not a POW, and therefore not entitled to the protections of Geneva III. This would seem to be just the type of situation Geneva III was designed to protect against. Because of the issues presented in connection with the General's further confinement and treatment, it seems appropriate -- even necessary -- to address the issue of Defendant's status. Articles 2, 4, and 5 of Geneva III establish the standard for determining who is a POW. Must this determination await some kind of formal complaint by Defendant or a lawsuit presented on his behalf? In view of the issues presently raised by Defendant, the Court thinks not.

---

[166] *See* Warren, *supra* note 58, at 58-59.
[167] *See id.*
[168] See id.
[169] See United States v. Noriega, 808 F.Supp. 791 (S.D.Fla. 1992). The change in official status did not have any effect on his prison sentence.
[170] *Id.* at 794.

Chapter 3

TREATMENT OF DETAINEES AT GUANTÁNAMO

The Department of Defense defends its treatment of the detainees at the Guantánamo Naval Station as fully complying with the principles of the Geneva Convention, causing some to question whether a change in the Administration's position as to whether and how the United States is bound to apply the Geneva Conventions would in any way change the treatment the detainees are receiving. They point out that the detainees are receiving some of the benefits accorded under the Conventions to protected persons, and are not suffering inhumane treatment. If there is no uncertainty that none of the detainees qualifies as POWs and their treatment would not change, they argue, then holding tribunals to determine each detainee's status would be largely symbolic and therefore a waste of resources. Critics of the policy respond that the U.S.' position regarding the inapplicability of the Geneva Conventions could be invoked as precedent to defend the poor human rights practices of other regimes, and it could lead to harsh treatment of U.S. service members who fall into enemy hands during this or any future conflict. Under their view, if the Administration can accomplish its goals by applying the GPW to determine by means of a competent tribunal which of the detainees is entitled to POW status, the foreign policy and humanitarian benefits would be worth the cost.

The perceived implications of granting POW status appear to have played a role in the decision-making process, with Administration officials emphasizing the detrimental impact of treating the detainees as POWs on the U.S.' ability to fight the war against terror. There is some controversy over whether the predicted problems would necessarily result from a change in policy. Some of the issues are discussed below.

INTERROGATION

One argument cited frequently in the press for denying POW status to the detainees is that the U.S. military would no longer be able to interrogate them in an effort to gain intelligence. The GPW requires prisoners to give only a few personal facts, including name, rank, and serial number. Most armies undoubtedly forbid their soldiers from divulging any more information than what is required; however, there is no prohibition against the detaining power asking for more information.[171] It is forbidden to use mental or physical coercion to extract information from prisoners,[172] but tactics such as trickery or promises of improved living conditions are not foreclosed. Article [173] of GPW provides that "[p]risoners of war who refuse to answer may not be threatened, insulted, or exposed to any unpleasant or disadvantageous treatment of any kind." Torture is not permitted in the case of any detainee, regardless of that person's status.[174]

Similar language was contained in the 1929 Geneva Convention.[175] Despite the reports of widespread abuse of prisoners of war at the hands of enemy interrogators, there is very little case precedent defining the boundaries of acceptable conduct. [176] A British military court convicted several German Luftwaffe officers of improperly interrogating British POWs[177] at a special interrogation camp, where it was charged the officers used excessive heating of cells in order to induce prisoners to give war information of a kind they were not bound by the Convention to disclose. The charges also alleged the officers had threatened prisoners that their

---

[171] See ICRC COMMENTARY, supra note 93, at 164.
[172] GPW art. 17.
[173] See LEVIE, supra note 23, at 108.
[174] GC art. 31 prohibits the use of physical or mental coercion to obtain information. See also Convention Against Torture and Other Cruel, Inhuman or Degrading Treatment or Punishment, Jun. 26, 1987, 1465 U.N.T.S. 85.
[175] Geneva Prisoners of War Convention of 1929 art. 5 stated in part: No pressure shall be exerted on prisoners to obtain information regarding the situation of their armed forces or their country. Prisoners who refuse to reply may not be threatened, insulted, or exposed to unpleasantness or disadvantages of any kind whatsoever.
[176] See POW DOCUMENTS, supra note 108, at 708.
[177] See Trial of Erich Killinger and Four Others, 3 LRTWC 67, excerpts reprinted in POW DOCUMENTS, supra note 108, doc. No. 70, at 291.

failure to provide sufficient answers could be seen by the Gestapo as evidence that the prisoners were saboteurs.[178] The military court expressed its agreement with the defense's position that interrogation was not unlawful under the Geneva Convention then in force, that obtaining information by trick was likewise not unlawful, and that interrogation of a wounded prisoner was not itself unlawful without evidence that methods used amounted to physical or mental ill-treatment.[179]

It appears to be a common practice for militaries to interrogate prisoners as soon as possible after capture to exploit their knowledge concerning tactical positions and plans.[180] There is no express right to counsel during such interrogation; however, the case may be different where the information sought is of the type that could incriminate the prisoner personally for any crime.[181] The GPW forbids the use of coercion to induce a POW to admit guilt, and POWs who are accused of crimes have the right to counsel.[182] It may thus be argued that POWs are entitled to some form of exclusionary rule to keep a forced confession from introduction into evidence at trial.

TRIAL AND PUNISHMENT

Trial and punishment of detainees may call for different procedural guidelines depending on the status of the detainee and whether the offense was committed prior to capture or during captivity. Further, there is a distinction between crimes and mere disciplinary violations with respect to the nature and severity of punishment permitted. The Geneva Conventions do not permit collective punishment without an individual determination of guilt, nor confinement without a hearing. [183]

The Bush Administration is reportedly considering whether it will prosecute membership in al Qaeda as a war crime, without the need to prove

---

[178] *See id.*
[179] *See id.* at 292.
[180] *See* ICRC COMMENTARY, *supra* note 93, at 163.
[181] *See* LEVIE, *supra* note 23, at 109, n42 (arguing the "interrogation of a prisoner of war in a search for tactical information of immediate urgency cannot be equated to the interrogation of an individual arrested for questioning in connection with the possible commission of a crime...").
[182] GPW art. 99 states in part: No moral or physical coercion may be exerted on a prisoner of war in order to induce him to admit himself guilty of the act of which he is accused. No prisoner of war may be convicted without having had an opportunity to present his defence and the assistance of a qualified advocate or counsel.
[183] *See* GPW art. 87; GC III art. 33.

unlawful acts.[184] The military has jurisdiction to try enemy POWs and civilians, including "unlawful belligerents," for violations of the law of war.[185] However, the military does not appear to have jurisdiction to try detainees for pre-capture acts not committed within occupied territory or in connection with the armed conflict, as described below.[186] The use of a conspiracy theory to try detainees for membership in al Qaeda could be problematic, possibly opening the convictions to collateral challenges as resulting from the application of *ex post facto* laws[187] or exceeding the constitutional prerogatives of the President.[188] The Administration points to the Nuremberg Charter as precedent for penalizing membership in a criminal organization,[189] but the Nuremberg tribunal sharply limited its application, finding guilt only in members of sufficiently high rank and with personal

---

[184] *See* Jess Bravin, *White House Lawyers Weigh Classifying Al Qaeda Membership as a War Crime*, WALL ST. J. Mar. 5, 2002, at A18, *available at* 2002 WL-WSJ 3387714 (quoting an unnamed official as stating, "[o]ne of the war crimes you could be able to prove . . . is close to a status offense, which is being a member of a global terrorist conspiracy.")

[185] *See* 10 U.S.C. § 821 (recognizing concurrent jurisdiction of military courts over offenders or offenses designated by statute or the law of war); 10 U.S.C. § 818 (recognizing courtsmartial jurisdiction over violations of the law of war committed by any person). For a brief overview comparing jurisdiction and procedure among various courts, see Selected Procedural Safeguards in Federal, Military, and International Courts, CRS Report RL31262, Jan. 30, 2002.

[186] For example, some of the detainees allegedly were arrested outside the zone of operations, in Bosnia, for suspicion of involvement in al Qaeda terrorist plots. Some observers believe they can only be charged as common criminals and not as unlawful belligerents.

[187] GPW art. 99 ("No prisoner of war may be tried or sentenced for an act which is not forbidden by the law of the Detaining Power or by international law, in force at the time the said act was committed.").

[188] *See* U.S. Const. Art. 1, § 8, cl.10 (empowering the Congress to define and punish offenses against the "Law of Nations").

[189] Agreement for the Prosecution and Punishment of the Major War Criminals of the European Axis (London Agreement) August 8, 1945, 58 Stat. 1544, 82 U.N.T.S. 280. Article 9. At the trial of any individual member of any group or organization the Tribunal may declare (in connection with any act of which the individual may be convicted) that the group or organization of which the individual was a member was a criminal organization. After the receipt of the Indictment the Tribunal shall give such notice as it thinks fit that the prosecution intends to ask the Tribunal to make such declaration and any member of the organization will be entitled to apply to the Tribunal for leave to be heard by the Tribunal upon the question of the criminal character of the organization. The Tribunal shall have power to allow or reject the application. If the application is allowed, the Tribunal may direct in what manner the applicants shall be represented and heard. Article 10. In cases where a group or organization is declared criminal by the Tribunal, the competent national authority of any Signatory shall have the right to bring individual to trial for membership therein before national, military or occupation courts. In any such case the criminal nature of the group or organization is considered proved and shall not be questioned.

knowledge or involvement in the actual crimes.[190] In any event, the Nuremberg tribunal had jurisdiction over the question of whether a charged organization was indeed criminal, and could hear evidence to the contrary proffered by any member of the group.

POWs

According to GPW article 102:

> A prisoner of war can be validly sentenced only if the sentence has been pronounced by the same courts according to the same procedure as in the case of members of the armed forces of the Detaining Power, and if, furthermore, the provisions of the present Chapter have been observed.

Further, Article 84 provides:

> In no circumstances whatever shall a prisoner of war be tried by a court of any kind which does not offer the essential guarantees of independence and impartiality as generally recognized, and, in particular, the procedure of which does not afford the accused the rights and means of defence provided for in Article 105.[191]

Other procedural guarantees under the GPW include a prohibition on punishment for *ex post facto* crimes,[192] prompt notification of the charges and a speedy trial,[193] notification to the Protecting Power of the impending trial at least three weeks in advance,[194] right to counsel of the POW's own

---

[190] *See* TELFORD TAYLOR, THE ANATOMY OF THE NUREMBERG TRIALS 584 (1992).

[191] *See infra* note 195.

[192] GPW art. 99.

[193] GPW art. 103 states: Judicial investigations relating to a prisoner of war shall be conducted as rapidly as circumstances permit and so that his trial shall take place as soon as possible. A prisoner of war shall not be confined while awaiting trial unless a member of the armed forces of the Detaining Power would be so confined if he were accused of a similar offence, or if it is essential to do so in the interests of national security. In no circumstances shall this confinement exceed three months.

[194] GPW art. 104 requires the following information to be reported to the Protecting Power (*see supra* note 48) and POW's representative before a trial can commence: 1. Surname and first names of the prisoner of war, his rank, his army, regimental, personal or serial number, his date of birth, and his profession or trade, if any; 2. Place of internment or confinement; 3. Specification of the charge or charges on which the prisoner of war is to be arraigned, giving the legal provisions applicable; 4 . Designation of the court which will

choosing or appointed counsel,[195] trial in the presence of a representative of the Protecting Power,[196] the right to appeal a decision,[197] and if convicted, the right to serve the sentence under humane conditions.[198] Special Provisions apply in case the offense is punishable by death. A POW sentenced to death may not be executed until six months after the Protecting Power has received the required notification under art. 107.[199] The court must be informed that

---

try the case; likewise the date and place fixed for the opening of the trial. The same communication shall be made by the Detaining Power to the prisoner's representative.

[195] GPW art. 105 provides: The prisoner of war shall be entitled to assistance by one of his prisoner comrades, to defence by a qualified advocate or counsel of his own choice, to the calling of witnesses and, if he deems necessary, to the services of a competent interpreter. He shall be advised of these rights by the Detaining Power in due time before the trial. Failing a choice by the prisoner of war, the Protecting Power shall find him an advocate or counsel, and shall have at least one week at its disposal for the purpose. The Detaining Power shall deliver to the said Power, on request, a list of persons qualified to present the defence. Failing a choice of an advocate or counsel by the prisoner of war or the Protecting Power, the Detaining Power shall appoint a competent advocate or counsel to conduct the defence.

The advocate or counsel conducting the defence on behalf of the prisoner of war shall have at his disposal a period of two weeks at least before the opening of the trial, as well as the necessary facilities to prepare the defence of the accused. He may, in particular, freely visit the accused and interview him in private. He may also confer with any witnesses for the defence, including prisoners of war. He shall have the benefit of these facilities until the term of appeal or petition has expired.

Particulars of the charge or charges on which the prisoner of war is to be arraigned, as well as the documents which are generally communicated to the accused by virtue of the laws in force in the armed forces of the Detaining Power, shall be communicated to the accused prisoner of war in a language which he understands, and in good time before the opening of the trial. The same communication in the same circumstances shall be made to the advocate or counsel conducting the defence on behalf of the prisoner of war.

The representatives of the Protecting Power shall be entitled to attend the trial of the case, unless, exceptionally, this is held in camera in the interest of State security. In such a case the Detaining Power shall advise the Protecting Power accordingly.

[196] *Id.* ("The representatives of the Protecting Power shall be entitled to attend the trial of the case, unless, exceptionally, this is held in camera in the interest of State security.").

[197] GPW art. 106: Every prisoner of war shall have, in the same manner as the members of the armed forces of the Detaining Power, the right of appeal or petition from any sentence pronounced upon him, with a view to the quashing or revising of the sentence or the reopening of the trial. He shall be fully informed of his right to appeal or petition and of the time limit within which he may do so.

[198] GPW art. 108: Sentences pronounced on prisoners of war after a conviction has become duly enforceable, shall be served in the same establishments and under the same conditions as in the case of members of the armed forces of the Detaining Power. These conditions shall in all cases conform to the requirements of health and humanity.

[199] GPW art. 101.

the POW owes no allegiance to the Detaining Power, encouraging the court to exercise leniency in sentencing on that basis.[200]

Civilians

A belligerent state may exercise jurisdiction over civilians in occupied territory subject to section III of the GC. However, the penal laws of the occupied territory remain in force unless the Occupying Power repeals or suspends them "in cases where they constitute a threat to its security or an obstacle to the application of the present Convention."[201] The Occupying Power may also institute such laws that are essential to maintaining order and security, and to carrying out its obligations under the GC,[202] but these may not be enforced retroactively.[203] In addition, "[n]o sentence shall be pronounced by the competent courts of the Occupying Power except after a regular trial."[204] All accused persons have the right to be "promptly informed, in writing, in a language which they understand, of the particulars of the charges preferred against them, and shall be brought to trial as rapidly as possible."[205] The accused has the right to counsel of choice and an interpreter, the right to present evidence necessary to his defense,[206] and the right to appeal a sentence.[207] These provisions apply not only in occupied territory but also, by analogy, to persons interned on the territory of the Detaining Power.[208]

Protected persons have the additional right to have the Protecting Power notified of the charges[209] and may have a representative of that power attend the trial.[210] If a protected person is sentenced to death, the sentence may not

---

[200] GPW art. 100.
[201] GC art. 64
[202] Id.
[203] See id. art. 65-66
[204] Id. art 71.
[205] Id.
[206] GC. art. 72.
[207] Id. art. 73.
[208] Id. art. 126 (applying arts. 71-76 by analogy to internees in the national territory of the Detaining Power). It is arguable that this provision would also encompass detainees at Guantánamo Bay, although the base is not technically U.S. territory.
[209] Id. art 71.
[210] Id. art 74.

be carried out prior to six months after the Protecting Power is notified of the sentence.[211]

Chapter IX applies to civilian internees, and provides protection against duplicate punishment.[212] Violations of camp disciplinary rules may also be punished, but they are not to be treated as crimes. Internees may not be punished for a simple disciplinary breach, including attempted escape,[213] by confinement in a penitentiary.[214]

Unlawful Belligerents

The term "unlawful belligerents" is not found in the Geneva Conventions. Therefore, rules applicable to the trials of unlawful belligerents depend on whether the person charged is considered to be a civilian or whether a separate standard, found outside of the Geneva Conventions, applies. If the minimum standards outlined in Common Article 3 apply, the following are forbidden:

> The passing of sentences and the carrying out of executions without previous judgment pronounced by a regularly constituted court, affording all the judicial guarantees which are recognized as indispensable by civilized peoples.

SECURITY MEASURES

Many nations impose upon their soldiers the duty to make every effort to escape from captivity if they should fall into the hands of the enemy.[215] At the same time, the Detaining Power will undoubtedly seek to take all possible precautions to prevent escape.[216] The Geneva Conventions regulate the use of deadly force to prevent an escape, requiring warning prior to the

---

[211] Id. art 75.
[212] Id.art. 118.
[213] GC art. 122.
[214] Id. art. 124.
[215] *See* LEVIE, *supra* note 23, at 403.
[216] *See id.* (noting POWs will likely be placed in enclosures made "as escape-proof as humanly possible").

firing of any shots.[217] Attempted escape or aiding and abetting such an attempt is treated as a disciplinary matter only; once an escape is deemed to be "successful," in the case the prisoner is recaptured, no punishment is permitted.[218] A prisoner who has attempted escape may be subjected to extraordinary surveillance measures.[219]

It is unclear where the line between security measures and punitive measures lies. POWs are entitled to living quarters similar to those of their guards.[220] In contrast, press reports have described the facilities at Guantánamo Bay as similar to a "high security prison." The present living conditions may be subject to criticism as punitive measures. However, it is recognized that POW camps as they are first established may not meet all of the requirements of the GPW. U.S. officials are reportedly building less temporary facilities that will provide more protection against the elements than the prisoners currently receive.

The Conventions allow prisoners to be searched and weapons confiscated, but personal property must be returned to them once internment ends.[221] U.S. Army regulations require detainees to be searched for weapons and other contraband immediately after their capture, prior to a determination of the captive's status.

REPATRIATION

One argument advanced to support denying POW status to the detainees is that the United States would be required to return them to their countries of origin once hostilities cease. Some observers argue that this may not be such an immediate requirement, and question whether hostilities will have ceased when U.S. troops have ceased combat operations in Afghanistan.

Under GPW art. 21, internment of POWs must cease when no longer necessary. According to GPW art. 118, repatriation must occur "without

---

[217] GPW art. 42 provides: The use of weapons against prisoners of war, especially against those who are escaping or attempting to escape, shall constitute an extreme measure, which shall always be preceded by warnings appropriate to the circumstances.

[218] *Id.* art. 91-95.

[219] GPW art. 92; GC art. 120.

[220] GPW art. 25 provides: Prisoners of war shall be quartered under conditions as favourable as those for the forces of the Detaining Power who are billeted in the same area. The said conditions shall make allowance for the habits and customs of the prisoners and shall in no case be prejudicial to their health.

[221] *See* LEVIE, *supra* note 23, at 110.

delay at the cessation of active hostilities." The language of the 1929 Geneva Convention has not been as adamant, requiring only that parties should provide, in armistice agreements, for repatriation of prisoners to occur "with the least possible delay after cessation of hostilities."[222] However, there is an exception for prisoners who are charged with or have been convicted of an indictable crime.[223] There is also case law suggesting the obligation to repatriate is not automatic and immediate. The 9th Circuit declined to grant freedom to a POW captured in Italy during the Second World War, who sought release partly on the grounds that hostilities had ceased.[224] The court noted that no peace treaty had yet been negotiated between Italy and the United States, and was not swayed by the fact that Italy had by that time changed sides. It appears to have remained international state practice to provide for repatriation of prisoners of war by express agreement.[225]

Interned civilians must also be released "as soon as the reasons which necessitated [their] internment no longer exist,"[226] which will occur "as soon as possible after the close of hostilities."[227] There is an exception for internees against whom penal proceedings are pending or who have been convicted and sentenced for non-disciplinary offenses.[228] These internees may be detained "until the close of such proceedings and, if circumstances require, until the completion of the penalty."[229]

RIGHT TO REDRESS

The proper treatment of prisoners is the responsibility of the detaining power and the individuals directly responsible for their conditions. Mistreatment of prisoners of war may incur liability under both international

---

[222] *See* 1929 Geneva Convention Relative to the Treatment of Prisoners of War art. 75, 47 Stat. 2021 (July 27, 1929).

[223] *See* GPW art. 119: Prisoners of war against whom criminal proceedings for an indictable offence are pending may be detained until the end of such proceedings, and, if necessary, until the completion of the punishment. The same shall apply to prisoners of war already convicted for an indictable offence.

[224] *See In re* Territo, 156 F.2d 142 (9th Cir. 1946).

[225] *See, e.g.* POW DOCUMENTS, *supra* note 108, at 796, (noting that it took nearly two years after hostilities between Pakistan and India ended in 1971 before Pakistani prisoners of war were repatriated).

[226] GC art. 132.

[227] *Id.* art. 133.

[228] GC art. 133.

[229] *Id.*

norms and the UCMJ. It is possible that the refusal to hold tribunals to determine the legal status and rights of detainees may also contravene the law of war.[230] Detainees have the right to protest their treatment to the detaining power or to a neutral power or organization serving as the protecting power,[231] and may not be punished for having asserted a grievance, even where it is considered unfounded.[232] (In this case, the role of protector appears to be filled by the International Committee of the Red Cross.) The detainees may also have recourse to federal courts to enforce their rights under the Geneva Conventions.[233] Other signatory states are obligated to "ensure respect" for the Conventions "in all circumstances,"[234] meaning that other states may issue diplomatic challenges on behalf of the detainees, and may even find a cause of action in domestic courts to challenge the detention.[235]

Whether the detainees will have the right to protest the legality of their detention itself likely depends on whether federal courts accept jurisdiction to hear petitions for *habeas corpus* brought on their behalf. One such petition was dismissed by a district court in California for lack of standing.[236] Another petition is currently under consideration in the U.S. District Court

---

[230] Failure to afford a prisoner a regular trial in accordance with the 1929 Geneva Convention resulted in some convictions by post-World War II tribunals. Japan, for example, adopted a policy proclaiming enemy airmen who participated in bombing raids against Japanese territory to be violators of the law of war and subject to execution. This "Enemy Airmen Act" resulted in the deaths of many captured American fliers after alledgedly sham trials. *See* Trial of Lieutenant General Shigeru Sawada and Three Others, 5 LRTWC 1 (U.S. Military Commission, Shanghai 1946), *reprinted in* POW DOCUMENTS, *supra* note 108, doc. no. 78 (four Japanese officers convicted of denying fair trial to captured "Doolittle Raiders"); Trial of Lieutenant General Harukei Isayama and Seven Others, 5 LRTWC 60 (U.S. Military Commission, Shanghai 1946), *reprinted in* POW DOCUMENTS, *supra* note 108, doc. no. 82 (conviction for "permitting and participating in an illegal and false trial" of American POWs).

[231] GPW art. 78.

[232] *Id.*

[233] *See* U.S. v. Noriega, 808 F.Supp.791 (S.D.Fla. 1992)(holding the GPW to be a selfexecuting treaty). *But see* Johnson v. Eisentraeger 339 U.S. 763 (1950) (denying petition for *habeas corpus* to alien enemies who had not entered U.S. territory).

[234] GPW art. 1.

[235] Such a suit was recently dismissed in Great Britain. *See* John Chapman, *'Taliban' Briton Loses His Court Bid*, DAILY EXPRESS (United Kingdom), Mar. 16, 2002, at 47. The mother of a British detainee brought a case claiming her son, one of the detainees held at Guantanamo Bay, has wrongly been denied POW status, was interrogated by British security services and has been denied legal representation. The High Court rejected the challenge as essentially a "political question."

[236] Coalition of Clergy v. Bush, No. CV 02-570 AHM (JTLX), 2002 WL 272428 (C.D. Cal. 2002).

for the District of Columbia.[237] The U.S. Justice Department has reportedly set up a special legal team headed by U.S. Solicitor-General Theodore Olson to oversee the government's cases against expected petitions brought by detainees and their representatives.[238]

The District Court in Los Angeles agreed with the Justice Department that the 1950 Supreme Court decision in *Johnson v. Eisentraeger*[239] forecloses its jurisdiction to hear a petition for *habeas corpus* because the detainees have never entered any territory under U.S. sovereignty.[240] In *Johnson*, the Supreme Court affirmed the convictions of German citizens who had been convicted by U.S. military commissions set up in China of carrying out belligerent acts after peace with Germany had been established. The Court held the federal courts did not have jurisdiction to hear the case because the writ of *habeas corpus* was not available to "enemy alien[s], who at no relevant time and in no stage of [their] captivity [have] been within [the court's] jurisdiction."[241] The Supreme Court noted further that:

> The privilege of litigation has been extended to aliens, whether friendly or enemy, only because permitting their presence in the country implied protection. No such basis can be invoked here, for these prisoners at no relevant time were within any territory over which the United States is sovereign and the circumstances of their offense [and] their capture ... were all beyond the territorial jurisdiction of any court of the United States.[242]

There are several distinguishing factors relative to the suit on behalf of the detainees in Cuba that may prove important if the determination comes before a federal court. First, the detainees are not "enemy aliens" in the same sense of the petitioners in *Johnson*, because they are not citizens of a hostile nation against whom Congress has declared war.[243] An enemy alien is

---

[237] *See* Cienski, *supra* note 13 (reporting that a petition was filed by the parents of detainees from Australia and the United Kingdom).

[238] *See* Mintz, *supra* note 11.

[239] 339 U.S. 763 (1950).

[240] *Coalition of Clergy* at 16. The court concluded that *Johnson* establishes that whether Guantánamo detainees "can establish jurisdiction in any district court depends not on the nature of their claims but on whether the Naval Base at Guantánamo Bay is under the sovereignty of the United States." *Id.* at 20.

[241] 339 U.S. 767.

[242] *Id.* at 777-78.

[243] *See Johnson* at 769 ("In the primary meaning of the words, an alien friend is the subject of a foreign state at peace with the United States; an alien enemy is the subject of a foreign state at war with the United States.")(citing Techt v. Hughes, 229 N.Y. 222, 229, 128 N.E. 185, 186, *cert.denied* 254 U.S. 643 (1920)).

defined by statute as all "natives, citizens, denizens, or subjects" of a hostile nation or government during time of declared war.[244] While the Enemy Alien Act pertains only to aliens residing or located within the United States, the *Johnson* Court relied in part on the authority of that Act to determine the legal disabilities of petitioner enemy aliens.[245]

Second, the *Johnson* petition challenged the jurisdiction of the military commission to try the petitioners for violations of the law of war, but did not challenge their status as enemy aliens. The detainees in Cuba, who have not been charged with any violation against the law of war or any other crime, presumably would challenge the detention itself.[246] The *Johnson* Court noted that the threshold question of status would be one for judicial determination:

> Courts will entertain [the enemy alien's] plea for freedom from Executive custody only to ascertain the existence of a state of war and whether he is an alien enemy and so subject to the Alien Enemy Act. Once these jurisdictional elements have been determined, courts will not inquire into any other issue as to his internment.[247]

Under similar analysis, the detainees at Guantánamo Bay would have access to federal courts at least to establish their status as enemy belligerents or POWs.

Third, the Geneva Conventions of 1949, not yet in force when *Johnson* was decided, may give the detainees enforceable rights to challenge their

---

[244] The Enemy Alien Act, 50 U.S.C.§ 21 provides: Whenever there is a declared war between the United States and any foreign nation or government, or any invasion or predatory incursion is perpetrated, attempted, or threatened against the territory of the United States by any foreign nation or government, and the President makes public proclamation of the event, all natives, citizens, denizens, or subjects of the hostile nation or government, being of the age of fourteen years and upward, who shall be within the United States and not actually naturalized, shall be liable to be apprehended, restrained, secured, and removed as alien enemies.

[245] 339 U.S. at 773. *See also* United States v. Tiede, 86 F.R.D. 227 (1979) (order granting Polish national right to a jury trial in non-Article III American court sitting in West Berlin; distinguishing *Johnson* based on alien enemy status of petitioners in that case).

[246] *See* 339 U.S. at 795. The *Johnson* Court expressly held "that the Constitution does not confer a right of personal security or an immunity from military trial and punishment upon an alien enemy engaged in the hostile service of a government at war with the United States." The detainees might argue that the indefinite detention of aliens who are neither prisoners of war nor charged with any crime is distinguishable from the case of admitted alien enemies charged and convicted for offenses.

[247] *Id.* at 775.

treatment.[248] The *Johnson* Court declined to take into consideration whether the petitioners had been tried in violation of the 1929 Geneva Convention on Prisoners of War based on its earlier interpretation that that Convention applied only to disciplinary offenses committed during capture and not to pre-capture violations of the law of war.[249] However, the 1949 Geneva Convention was drafted to clarify that it applies to trials for any offense, whether committed during or prior to internment.[250]

---

[248] *See* U.S. v. Noriega, 808 F.Supp.791, 797-99 (S.D.Fla..1992)(affirming Noriega's right to enforce POW rights in federal court).

[249] 339 U.S. at 789-90 (citing *Ex parte* Quirin, 317 U.S. 1, 37 (1941); *In re* Yamashita, 327 U.S. 1 (1946)).

[250] *See* LEVIE, *supra* note 23, at 379-80.

Chapter 4

CONGRESS' ROLE

The Constitution provides Congress with ample authority to legislate the treatment of battlefield detainees in the custody of the U.S. military. The Constitution empowers Congress to make rules regarding capture on land or water,[251] to define and punish violations of international law,[252] and to make regulations to govern the armed forces.[253] Congress also has the constitutional prerogative to declare war,[254] a power it has not yet exercised with regard to the armed conflict in Afghanistan. By not declaring war, Congress has implicitly limited some presidential authorities.[255]

Despite the constitutional powers listed above, Congress has not generally taken an active rule in prescribing the treatment of prisoners of war. Existing statutes concerning enemy prisoners of war are limited to providing for the use of DoD funds to pay expenses incident to the maintenance, pay, and allowances of persons in custody of any military department,[256] to provide for the disposition of the remains of enemy prisoners of war and interned enemy aliens who die in the custody of a military department,[257] to penalize those who aid the escape of an enemy prisoner,[258] and to exempt prisoners of war from the entitlement to claim of

---

[251] U.S. CONST. art. I, § 8, cl. 11
[252] *Id.* art. I, § 8, cl. 10.
[253] *Id.* art. I, § 8, cl. 14.
[254] *Id.* art. I, § 8, cl. 11.
[255] *See* Declarations of War and Authorizations for the Use of Military Force: Background and Legal Implications, CRS Report RL31133 (Sept. 27, 2001).
[256] 10 U.S.C. § 956(5).
[257] 10 U.S.C. § 1483.
[258] 18 U.S.C. § 757.

compensation for injury or death resulting from war-risk hazard.[259] However, prisoners of war are covered under the jurisdiction of the Uniform Code of Military Justice (UCMJ).[260] The UCMJ does not indicate whether detainees who are determined not to be prisoners of war are covered.

The Administration has asserted that the war on terror is a new kind of conflict, requiring a new set of rules and definitions. It has been observed that the nature of the hostilities and U.S. objectives borrow some characteristics from the realm of law enforcement and others from a model based on conventional war. Consequently, the role of Congress might be seen as particularly important in providing a definition and a set of boundaries to shape how such a war is to be fought.

Congress' role may take on greater importance in the event that federal courts decline jurisdiction to hear challenges by the detainees. As the Supreme Court noted in *Johnson v. Eisentraeger*, its holding was not

> that these prisoners have no right which the military authorities are bound to respect. The United States, by the [1949] Geneva Convention ... concluded an agreement upon the treatment to be accorded captives. These prisoners claim to be and are entitled to its protection. It is, however, the obvious scheme of the Agreement that responsibility for observance and enforcement of these rights is upon political and military authorities. Rights of alien enemies are vindicated under it only through protests and intervention of protecting powers as the rights of our citizens against foreign governments are vindicated only by Presidential intervention.[261]

---

[259] 42 U.S.C. § 1701.
[260] *See* 10 U.S.C. § 802(a)(9).
[261] Johnson v. Eisentraeger, 339 U.S. 763, 789 (1950).

INDEX

A

accused, viii, 4, 29, 39, 41-43
acts of violence, viii, 4, 25
Afghanistan, 4, 16, 19-23, 28, 30, 45, 51
al Qaeda, vii, 1, 5, 6, 16, 17, 21-24, 27, 39, 40
alien enem(y)ies, 47-49, 52
Alien Enemy Act, 49
armed conflict, vii, 3, 7, 9, 10, 15, 17-21, 25, 30, 33, 35, 40, 51
armed forces, vii, 3-5, 10, 14-16, 20-24, 27, 29-31, 34-36, 38, 41, 42, 51
Army Regulation (AR), 12, 35
attempted escape, 44, 45

B

belligerent acts, viii, 3, 9, 13, 16, 17, 35, 48
Bush Administration, 39
Bush, President, vii, 1, 3, 33

C

camps, 45
captive's status, 35, 45
captives, 2, 5, 52
captivity, 9, 10, 12, 39, 44, 48
case law, 46
chaplains, 35
civil convictions, 23
civil court, 4
civil trial, 13
Civil War, 11
civilian internees (CI), 35, 44
civilians, viii, 3, 6, 9, 12, 13, 16, 18, 24, 26, 28, 32, 40, 43, 46
combat operations, 12, 16, 45
compensation, 15, 52
contraband, 45
conventional war, 52
criminal convictions, 23
criminal trial, 11
Cuba, vii, 1, 2, 48, 49

D

dead, 15, 32
deadly force, 44
destruction, 10, 29, 32
detaining power, 2, 9, 12, 40-45
disciplinary breach, 44
disciplinary matter, 45
drug charges, 36

E

Enemy Alien Act, 49
enemy alien(s), 3, 48, 49, 51
enemy belligerents, 49
enemy combatants, 9, 12, 21, 28
enemy interrogators, 38
enemy prisoner(s), 51
enemy prisoners of war (EPW(s)), 35
escape, 10, 30, 44, 45, 51
European Parliament, 2

F

fair trial, 10, 47
Field Manual (FM), 11, 12, 14, 27-29, 31, 34, 35
fixed distinctive sign, viii, 3, 28, 31
foreign policy, 37

G

general courts-martial, 35
Geneva Convention for the Treatment of Prisoners of War (GPW), vii, 2-5, 8-12, 14, 18-26, 28, 33, 35-43, 45-47
Geneva Convention(s) (GC), vii, viii, 1-6, 8-21, 32, 34, 37-39, 43, 44-47, 49, 50, 52
Geneva law, 7
government-in-exile, 23
Great Britain, 2, 47
grievance, 47
Guantánamo Bay, vii, 1, 2, 43, 45, 48, 49
Guantánamo Naval Station, 37
guerrilla tactics, 17, 30

H

habeas corpus, 3, 47, 48
Hague law, 7
handling of prisoners, 12

hostile activities, 24, 34, 35
hostilities, 4, 8-10, 12, 13, 15-20, 26, 29, 31, 45, 46, 52
human rights organizations, vii, 1, 2
human rights, vii, 1, 3, 7, 18, 19, 36, 37
humanitarian, 7, 9, 19, 20, 28, 33, 36, 37

I

improper conduct, 32
independent tribunal, vii, 2
indictable crime, 46
inhumane treatment, 37
injury or death, 52
intelligence, 28, 30, 35, 38
internal armed conflict, 19
international armed conflict, 19, 20, 35
International Committee of the Red Cross (ICRC), 2, 10, 20, 30-32, 34, 38, 39
international norms, 47
international obligations, 2
international personality, 6
international standards, vii, 1
interpreters, 35
interrogation camp, 38
Israeli court, 23

J

Jordan, 23
judicial guarantees, 19, 44
Justice Department, 3, 48

L

law(s) of war, viii, 3-9, 11, 13, 16-22, 24, 26, 27, 29-33, 40, 47, 49, 50
lawful belligerents, 13
lawful combatants, vii, 1, 10, 22, 26, 29, 30

legal status, vii, 2, 18, 19, 47
legality, 7, 47
Lieber Code, 11, 24
living quarters, 45

M

medical personnel, 35
mercenaries, 13, 15, 16
Military Assistance Command (MACV), 34
military court, 38
Military Operations Other than War (MOOTW), 35
military tribunal, 13
militias, vii, 3, 21, 26, 29, 31
Mistreatment of prisoners, 46
moral criteria, 32

N

non-disciplinary offenses, 46
Noriega, General Manuel, 35, 36, 47, 50
North Vietnamese Army, 34
Nuremberg Charter, 40

O

occupied territory, 12, 14, 23, 35, 40, 43
occupying power, 6, 14, 15, 43
Operation Just Cause, 19, 36
Organization of American States' Inter-American Commission, vii, 2
organized resistence forces, vii, 3, 21
other detainees (OD), 35

P

Panama, 19, 35, 36
partisan group, 23, 24
penalty, 35, 46
Pentagon, 16, 30

personal property, 45
pillage, 32
Popular Front for the Liberation of Palestine (PFLP), 23
Presidential intervention, 52
prisoners of war (POW), vii, viii, 1-6, 9-14, 16-18, 21-26, 29, 31-42, 44-47, 49-52
prisoners, vii, 1, 3, 6-12, 17, 29, 31, 33, 35, 38, 39, 42, 45, 46, 48, 49, 51, 52
protected persons, 6, 9, 12, 37
protecting power, 10, 41, 42, 43

R

Red Cross, 2, 19, 20, 35, 47
regular trial, 10, 14, 15, 43, 47
responsible command element, 27
retained personnel, 35
right to counsel, 39, 41, 43
right to redress, 46
rules of engagement (ROE), 7, 12.
Rumsfeld, Secretary, 1, 24, 27

S

saboteurs, 13, 14, 22, 24, 39
Second World War, 25, 46
security measures, viii, 4, 45
Solicitor-General, 2, 48
spies, 13, 14, 22, 24
status of the detainee, 39
Supreme Court, 3, 48, 52

T

Taliban, vii, 1, 4, 16, 17, 19-22, 24, 26, 27, 30, 47
terror, 37, 52
treatment of detainees, vii, 3, 9, 16
trial and punishment, 39
trial by court-martial, 4
tribunals, 34, 37, 47

U

U.N. High Commissioner on Human Rights (UNHCR), vii, 2
U.S. Justice Department, 2, 48
U.S. military, 12, 27, 38, 48, 51
Uniform Code of Military Justice (UCMJ), 14, 47, 52
unlawful belligerents, 13, 16, 17, 40, 44
unlawful combatants, viii, 4, 17, 18, 22, 30, 33, 36
unnecessary violence, 32
urgent measures, vii, 2

V

Vietcong prisoners, 33
Vietnam, 5, 33, 34
volunteer corps, vii, 3, 21, 25, 27-29, 31

W

war crime(s), 20, 31, 39, 40
weapons, 24, 31, 32, 45
West Bank, 23
wounded, 19, 31, 39
written provisions, 32